W9-AYA-503

Friends Always

The NEW Y-Indian Guide Programs Manual

YMCA of the USA

Cover Design and Layout: Conundrum Designs
Cover Photo: Marilyn Larsen/Berg and Associates

Copyright © 1988 YMCA of the USA
Published for the YMCA of the USA by Human Kinetics Publishers, Inc.

ISBN: 0-87322-133-8

Printed in the United States of America

10   9   8   7   6   5   4

Copies of this book may be purchased from the YMCA Program Store, Box 5077,
Champaign, IL 61825-5077, (217) 351-5077.

Contents

Preface

"Friends Always" captures the essence of Y-Indian Guide Programs—the opportunity to strengthen parent-child relationships through activities that are challenging and fun! Y-Indian Guide Programs are aimed at both parents and their five- to nine-year-old children. Parent-child pairs meet in small groups called "tribes," which get together regularly for planned events and outings. Activities are often based on an American Indian theme, a theme that stimulates creative projects and activities through which relationships are enhanced for a lifetime. This theme should always be used with great respect and dignity.

In these and in all other YMCA programs there are common goals for individuals and families, such as personal growth, appreciation of diversity in thought and traditions, and development of leadership skills. Such programs provide opportunities for accomplishing these essential goals.

This handbook offers a wealth of information on Y-Indian Guide Programs to enhance the experience for you and your child. The beginning section, Program Framework, provides an introduction to the programs and an explanation of what you can expect when you join a tribe. This is followed by the Indian Theme section, in which the Indian culture and its relationship to the programs is described. The Invitations section contains ideas for tribal meeting invitations, while the Tribal Property section consists of directions on how to create gear and costuming for tribal use. The large Crafts section is full of activity ideas for meetings and includes a list of additional resources. Other fun tribal meeting activities are covered in the sections on Games, Stories, Songs, and Family Activities. Addresses for further resources can be found in the Appendix.

The contents of this manual can get your tribe off to a good start. Add your enthusiasm and active participation to help build a relationship that will make you and your child "Friends Always."

Acknowledgments

This manual was developed for use by all Y-Indian Guide parents and participants. It contains information and ideas from many sources.

Development of the manual was coordinated by George Leinard, past National Y-Indian Guide Chief, with help from members of the National Program Council, who provided feedback and advice. The final manuscript was written by Sue Baugh; developmental editing was done by Patricia Sammann. Thanks go to Buena Washburn for carefully reviewing the Crafts section.

A special thanks to the YMCAs of Los Angeles, St. Paul, and Minneapolis for their permission to use text and art collected or developed by the Y-Indian Guide programs.

List of Invitations

List of Tribal Property

List of Crafts

List of Games

List of Stories

List of Songs

List of Family Activities

Program Framework

The Y-Indian Guide Programs have a long history of providing children between the ages of five and nine and their parents with opportunities for good times, learning, and mutual understanding. In this program you and your child will meet with other parent-child teams in a small group, called a tribe, to hold tribal meetings or participate in fun and educational outside activities. This Program Framework section contains a review of the basic ideas behind the Y-Indian Guide Programs, a description of how the programs work, and an explanation of how a typical tribal meeting is conducted. It also includes tips for beginning a new tribe and guidelines for program evaluation.

WHAT ARE THE Y-INDIAN GUIDE PROGRAMS?

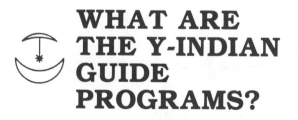

From small beginnings, the Y-Indian Guide Programs have grown to serve many thousands of people. This section starts with a discussion of the programs' origins and Indian theme. A short description of each of the four program branches is followed by the overall program objectives and a review of the characteristics of children in the Y-Indian Guide Programs age group.

How YMCA Indian Guide Programs Began

The first Y-Indian Guide Program was developed to support parents' vital role as teachers, counselors, and friends to their children. Harold S. Keltner, St. Louis YMCA Director, initiated the program as an integral part of Association work. In 1926, he organized the first tribe in Richmond Heights, Missouri, with the help of his good friend, Joe Friday, an Ojibway Indian, and William H. Hefelfinger, chief of the first Y-Indian Guide tribe. Inspired by his experiences with Joe Friday, who was his guide on fishing and hunting trips into Canada, Harold Keltner established a program of parent-child experiences that now involves several hundred thousand children and adults annually in the YMCA.

Joe Friday planted the seed for this program during a hunting trip he and Mr. Keltner took to Canada. One evening, the Ojibway said to his white colleague as they sat around a blazing campfire: "The Indian father raises his son. He teaches his son to hunt, to track, to fish, to walk softly and silently in the forest, to know the meaning and purpose of life and all he must know, while the white man allows the mother to raise his son." These comments struck home, and Harold Keltner arranged for Joe Friday to work with him at the St. Louis YMCA.

The Ojibway Indian spoke before groups of YMCA boys and their fathers in St. Louis, and Mr. Keltner discovered that fathers, as well as boys, had a keen interest in the traditions and ways of the American Indian. At the same time, Harold Keltner, being greatly influenced by the work of Ernest Thompson Seton, great lover of the out-of-doors, conceived the idea of a father-and-son program based upon the strong qualities of American Indian culture and life—dignity, patience, endurance, spirituality, harmony with nature, and concern for the family. Thus the first Y-Indian Guide program was born more than half a century ago.

3

The rise of the family YMCA following World War II, the genuine need for supporting little girls in their personal growth, and the demonstrated success of the father-son program nurtured the development of YMCA parent-daughter groups. The mother-daughter program, now called Y-Indian Maidens, was established in South Bend, Indiana, in 1951. Three years later, father-daughter groups, now known as Y-Indian Princesses, emerged in the Fresno, California YMCA. In 1980, the National Longhouse recognized the Y-Indian Braves Program for mothers and sons, thus completing the four programs and combinations in Y-Indian Guide Programs.

Although some Y-Indian Guide groups had extended their father-son experiences beyond the first three school grades from the beginning, it was not until 1969 that Y-Trail Blazers was recognized by the National Longhouse Executive Committee for nine- to eleven-year-old boys and their fathers. Trail Maidens, Trail Mates, and Coed Trail Blazers also have been developed and recognized in YMCAs across the country. Some YMCAs have created parent-child programs similar to those listed above but have oriented the program around a non-Indian theme. In the future, the YMCA hopes that expansion of these parent-child groups will continue as a positive force in strengthening family life.

The American Indian Theme

The Y-Indian Guide Programs can present parent-child teams—as well as families—with opportunities for new insights into the significant contributions Native American people have made to our nation's history and heritage. The past and present cultures of the American Indians can challenge a father or mother to be aware of his or her role as parent, guide, friend, and example for a son or daughter and help develop the child's natural curiosity and enthusiasm.

The teaching of values, attitudes, fitness and health, knowledge, and ethics to children is an integral part of the Indian way of life. At the same time, the Native American people feel a profound responsibility for the well-being of all family members. The sharing of food and clothing with all is a natural response for them whenever the need arises.

The American Indian culture gives the non-Indian parent a common interest and learning experience in working with his or her child. The genuine concern among Indian people for parent responsibility in teaching and guiding children to adulthood is a fine standard for all parents and children to live by today.

The American Indians have exceptional poise, dignity, and pride. Honesty and the given word have been inviolate in their way of life. Indians place a high priority on things of the spirit as opposed to a strictly material existence. Their deep appreciation for the Creator is apparent throughout their religion, traditions, and way of life. In addition, their understanding of the interdependence of the forces of nature is highly significant. All parents and children can recognize the great value of conserving resources and eliminating waste in our urban-centered world.

Through the purposeful parent-child experience of Y-Indian Guide Programs, the YMCA can be instrumental in upgrading the image of American Indians by supporting their self-pride, aiding the struggle to preserve their history, and recognizing their meaningful contribution to society.

The Four Branches of Y-Indian Guides

There are now four Y-Indian Guide Programs: Y-Indian Guides for fathers and sons; Y-Indian Princesses for fathers and daughters; Y-Indian Maidens for mothers and daughters; and Y-Indian Braves for mothers and sons. On the following pages the purpose, slogan, aims, and headband for each branch are described.

Y-INDIAN GUIDE PROGRAM

Purpose

The purpose of the Y-Indian Guide Program is to foster understanding and companionship between father and son.

Slogan

"Pals Forever"
The slogan, "Pals Forever," does *not* mean that father and son relate to each other as equals, such as two boys who are pals. Rather, it means that father and son have a close, enduring relationship in which there is communication, understanding, and companionship. The Y-Indian Guide Program encourages such a relationship by providing a means for father and son to share enjoyable experiences, to observe and learn about one another, and to develop mutual respect.

Aims

1. To be clean in body and pure in heart.
2. To be pals forever with my father/son.
3. To love the sacred circle of my family.
4. To listen while others speak.
5. To love my neighbor as myself.
6. To seek and preserve the beauty of the Great Spirit's work in forest, field, and stream.

Pledge

"We, father and son, through friendly service to each other, to our family, to this tribe, to our community, seek a world pleasing to the eye of the Great Spirit."

Headband

The central theme of the headband is the eye of the Great Spirit surrounded by the four winds of heaven. The feathered arrow designs that extend right and left from the central symbol represent the useful services of father and son. Among the American Indians, whenever someone achieved an outstanding feat, its significance was recognized by the Indian tribe, often in the form of feathers. The fact that the father-and-son achievements are united in the center of the design is interpreted to mean that fathers and sons together, under the eye of the Great Spirit, are seeking to help each other in the services they render.

On the right side of the headband are the symbols of the mother and the home. A line connects the mother symbol to home, which is symbolized by the fire in the tepee. On the left are symbols of father and son. Their relationship is represented by the line that joins the two symbols. These symbols add to the richness of the central theme, for it is in service to mother and home that many of the more significant achievements of father and son will take place.

Far to the right are symbols of day and forest. Far to the left are symbols of mountain, lake, field, and stream, with the moon for night. These symbols enrich the central theme, giving broader scope to services by centering the efforts of father and son on village and community life, and, as the aim states, "in forest, field, and stream."

Y-INDIAN PRINCESS PROGRAM

Purpose

The purpose of the Y-Indian Princess Program is to foster the understanding and companionship between father and daughter.

Slogan

"Friends Always"

Aims

1. To be clean in body and pure in heart.
2. To be friends always with my father/daughter.
3. To love the sacred circle of my family.
4. To listen while others speak.
5. To love my neighbor as myself.
6. To seek and preserve the beauty of the Great Spirit's work in forest, field, and stream.

Pledge

"We, father and daughter, through friendly service to each other, to our family, to this tribe, to our community, seek a world pleasing to the eye of the Great Spirit."

Headband

The central theme of the headband is the sign of the eye of the Great Spirit with the crossed arrows of friendship on the left side and the circled heart of love on the right side. The symbols for father and daughter are next to the grouped tepees, which indicate happy work in the community, and the single tepee, which denotes happy work in the home. The trees, water, and grass exhort the wearer to see and preserve the Great Spirit's beauty in forest, field, and stream.

Y-INDIAN MAIDEN PROGRAM

Purpose

The purpose of the Y-Indian Maiden Program is to foster the understanding and companionship between mother and daughter.

Slogan

"Friends Always"

Aims

1. To be clean in body and pure in heart.
2. To be friends always with my mother/daughter.
3. To love the sacred circle of my family.
4. To listen while others speak.
5. To love my neighbor as myself.
6. To seek and preserve the beauty of the Great Spirit's work in forest, field, and stream.

Pledge

"We, mother and daughter, through friendly service to each other, to our family, to this tribe, to our community, seek a world pleasing to the eye of the Great Spirit."

Headband

The central theme of the headband is the sign of the eye of the Great Spirit with the crossed arrows of friendship on one side and the circled heart of love on the other. The symbols of mother and daughter are next to the grouped tepees, which indicate happy work in the community, and the single tepee, which denotes happy work in the home. The trees, water, and grass exhort the wearer to see and preserve the Great Spirit's beauty in forest, field, and stream.

Y-INDIAN BRAVE
PROGRAM

Purpose

The purpose of the Y-Indian Brave Program is to foster the understanding and companionship between mother and son.

Slogan

"Friends Always"

Aims

1. To be clean in body and pure in heart.
2. To be friends always with my mother/son.
3. To love the sacred circle of my family.
4. To listen while others speak.
5. To love my neighbor as myself.
6. To seek and preserve the beauty of the Great Spirit's work in forest, field, and stream.

Pledge

"We, mother and son, through friendly service to each other, to our family, to this tribe, to our community, seek a world pleasing to the eye of the Great Spirit."

Headband

The central theme of the headband is the sign of the eye of the Great Spirit surrounded by the four winds of heaven. The feathered-arrow design on each side represents the useful service of mother and son. Mother and son stand to the left next to the single tepee, symbolizing mutual support in a happy home. To the right is a group of tepees symbolizing happy work in the community. The water, trees, mountains, and sky exhort the wearer to preserve the Great Spirit's beauty in forest, field, and stream.

Objectives of YMCA Indian Guide Programs

The YMCA locally, nationally, and internationally is dedicated to providing good opportunities for people to achieve their greatest and most satisfying potential as caring, responsible human beings. Y-Indian Guide Programs help fulfill this mission when they provide the following benefits to parents and children:

- Foster companionship and understanding and set a foundation for positive, lifelong relationships between parent and child.
- Build a sense of self-esteem and personal worth.
- Expand awareness of body, mind, and spirit.
- Provide the framework to meet a mutual need of spending enjoyable, constructive, and quality time together.
- Enhance the quality of family time.
- Emphasize the vital role that parents play in the growth and development of their children.
- Offer an important and unique opportunity to develop and enjoy volunteer leadership skills.

The Five- to Nine-Year-Old

Although all five- to nine-year-olds are not the same, they do share some general characteristics in their development. Considering these suggestions can help you understand your child and, along with other parents in your tribe, plan activities that are appropriate to the ages of your children.

Developmental Tasks

The YMCA program goals for five- to nine-year-olds are based on the developmental tasks of helping children to

- develop a growing confidence that they are liked and accepted by adults close to them;
- feel secure in their parents' love and be able to share some of this love with others;
- develop a sense of personal worth within the family, feeling responsible for tasks and for others;
- find increasing satisfaction in playing with others their own age and in sharing their possessions;

- develop identification with their fathers/mothers and a growing pride in being male/female;
- derive increasing satisfaction from physical skill development and active play;
- become useful in their homes and share in household tasks;
- find something they can do well and on their own;
- develop a growing appreciation of the need for rules and the ability to take direction; and
- accept and value each person for himself or herself.

Family Relationships

Positive relationships within the family provide a pattern for relationships with others outside the home. Y-Indian Guide Programs are designed to strengthen families by improving ties between parent and child. It is important, however, to consider the entire family as you make plans for the tribe. The following hints may be helpful:

- Provide opportunities for the rest of the family to be involved (such as designing several events for the families).
- Do craft projects in tribal meetings to give to other family members.
- Occasionally include family happenings as a part of scouting reports.
- Consider the rest of the family when scheduling tribal outings/events. For example, avoid scheduling a trip for parent and child on Mom's/Dad's birthday.
- Occasionally schedule activities for Mom and Dad away from the children, such as a dinner for tribal parents and their spouses.
- Use communication games in tribal meetings and encourage members to repeat the games at home with the rest of the family.

You'll find many additional activities to strengthen family relationships in the "Family Activities" section of this book.

Spiritual Development

Parents and family are the primary source of children's spiritual development. The five- to nine-year-olds are often curious about spiritual concerns, and parents can do much to help children's questioning minds by offering clear and honest explanations. Children of this age group observe and imitate their parents, who serve as models in developing a positive attitude toward people of different backgrounds and in gaining a sense of appreciation and reverence for God as Creator and source of comfort, strength, and power.

 # PROGRAM DESCRIPTION

If you are new to the Y-Indian Guide Programs, you will want to read the beginning of this section, where the overall organizational structure is explained. This section also provides information on tribal activities and both parents' and children's responsibilities within the programs.

Program Structure

Every participant in a Y-Indian Guide Program is also a part of the YMCA movement, which is active throughout the United States and in ninety-one countries around the world. Each Y-Indian Guide Program is organized through a local Y, and the YMCA director remains in contact with each tribe. Several levels of organization exist, beginning with the primary unit, the tribe.

Tribes

All Y-Indian Guide members participate in small neighborhood groups called *tribes*. A tribe usually consists of seven to ten parent-child teams. They meet at each others' homes regularly throughout the school year for program activities. Tribes elect a Chief and other officers, plan their own events, and conduct projects. The parents meet several times a year to develop plans and address problems.

Nations

Tribes may be affiliated with other tribes as part of a Y-Indian Guide *Nation*. A Nation may be any number of tribes grouped by YMCA branch, participant age, neighborhood, or other criteria. The tribal chiefs and Nation representatives (one parent from each tribe) usually meet each month to plan events in which all tribes may participate, such as a camp-out. Ideas are exchanged on tribal activi-

ties, stories, games, and the like, which helps promote tribal morale and strength.

Federations

Some YMCAs organize *Federations*, which are groups of several Nations. The term *Federation* also may refer to all Y-Indian Guide participants in a single YMCA.

Longhouses

Longhouse is an Indian term meaning "meeting" or "conference." A *Nation Longhouse* is a gathering of all participants in a particular Y-Indian Guide Nation. A *Federation Longhouse* is for all participants in that Federation. Some YMCAs organize a *Chief's Longhouse* that includes the heads of tribes (or Nations) in program planning.

The National Y-Indian Guide Longhouse

The National Y-Indian Guide Longhouse is a committee of the Program Services Division of the YMCA of the USA. Its purpose is to follow trends, provide support to local programs when requested, facilitate training for volunteers and staff at cluster and regional levels, assist with the development of program resources, and select the host and site for a national convention. Currently the National Longhouse structure includes the National Advisory Committee, Field Program Committees in some fields, and a National Program Council.

Tribal Activities

Each tribe has two or more tribal activities a month, at least one of which is a tribal meeting. The others may be either meetings or outside activities. Several times a year large intertribal events are held also.

The Tribal Meeting

Meetings are held in the homes of members on a rotating basis. A typical tribal meeting includes the following:

- Ceremonies such as opening and closing rituals (see "Tribal Rituals" section on pages 21-23).
- Activities such as crafts, stories, Indian lore, games, songs, and service projects.
- Refreshments provided by the host family.

Tribal meetings start and end on time and generally do not last longer than 1½ hours. Business and planning activities are kept to a minimum, as these can be taken care of during parents' meetings (described later).

The following are some sample activities for tribal meetings:

Cooking projects	Valucs discussions
Safety/first aid education	Health/fitness education
Ecology projects	Treasure hunts
Dress-up nights	Craft projects
Communication exercises	Gift making
	Backyard carnivals

You should plan activities that are easy for both children and parents to understand. Parent-child pairs should work as a team whenever possible. Try to use discussion activities and experiences, as well as crafts, as part of your tribal meetings.

Refreshments are served prior to the closing ritual or prayer, which is the official ending of the meeting. Parents and children sit together during refreshments as well as during the rest of the meeting to avoid breaking the tribe up into separate groups of parents and children.

Outside Activities

A key to the success of a tribe is the planning of varied outside activities, some examples of which are included in the following lists. Consult your YMCA Director for additional information and assistance.

Tribal Outings

Historic sites/parks	Airport
Museums	Tours of industries
Roller-skating	Restaurants
Ice-skating	Observatory
Zoo	Picnics
Boat/train trips	Sports events
Aquarium	Bakery
Movies and theaters	

Tribal Projects

Service projects	Scrapbook
Costumes/tribal property	Family involvement
Tribal plaque	Photo album

Other YMCA Programs

Call your YMCA for information on any of the following:

Y-Trail Blazers, Mates, Maidens, and Coed Trail Blazers (for older children)	Saturday gym and swim
	Fitness programs for adults, children, and families
Swimming lessons	Special interest classes
Gymnastics	
Day and resident camping	Service groups

Intertribal and Family Activities

The Longhouse or Nation usually will sponsor large intertribal events several times during the year. The following are some possible activities:

Induction ceremony	Swim/gym at the YMCA
Camp-outs	
Sledding/ice-skating	Family picnic
Special trips	Bowling
Pinewood derby	Bike rodeo
Kite flying	Christmas party
Slo-pitch softball	Banquet
Beach party	

Such activities also lend themselves to including families as well as the parents and children involved in the program. Although the primary purpose of the Y-Indian Guide Programs is to provide opportunities to strengthen and foster individual parent-child relationships, the parent and child are often part of a larger family group. You can involve other family members in tribal, nation, or federation activities in the following ways:

- Create and deliver tribal meeting invitations as a family project.
- Include all family members on outings such as hayrides or picnics.
- Hold a potluck supper to end the year.
- Sponsor a Family Day at a sports event.
- Have the child in the program teach or adapt a program activity to the rest of the family.
- Invite one other family in the tribe to be a

part of special occasions such as holidays and celebrations.

- Discuss values learned in the program at the family table.

Parents' Responsibilities

Parents' foremost responsibility in the Y-Indian Guide Programs is attending meetings with their children. Y-Indian Guide Programs are not children's programs but rather parent-child programs. Their purpose is to foster the companionship of parents with their children.

Parents also are expected to attend parents' meetings for long-range planning of tribal activities, to hold offices in the tribe, and to help with the crafting of tribal property.

Parents' Meetings

Most of the common shortcomings of tribes can be eliminated by meeting without the children several times during the year. The main purpose of these meetings is to iron out tiresome business details and avoid boring the children during tribal meetings. Any business that takes more than five minutes in a tribal meeting should be referred to the parents' meeting. Planning for trips, special events, and so forth goes much smoother when parents meet alone.

Advance planning can be done for a month or semester at a time at a parents' meeting. Also, the parents with logical excuses for not doing a certain task can explain their reasons without having the children present. Special events or surprises can be discussed without exciting the children too far ahead of time. For example, a weekend camping trip two months away can be planned by the parents without making the children wait too long.

Parents' meetings also offer excellent opportunities for learning. Tribal meetings can be evaluated, improvements suggested, and weak points discussed objectively by the parents alone. This is the most appropriate time for your Y Director or your organizer to listen to your problems and help you solve them.

Your time in the parents' meeting is best spent trying to understand your own child bet-

ter, learning how to be a closer pal and friend to your son or daughter, or trying to learn to cope with behavior problems. Although the Y is ready to help in this regard, often considerable understanding can be gained by a frank discussion of issues and problems among parents.

At these parents' meetings, you will have a chance to review the program manuals or books and magazine articles that will help you to be a better parent and program participant. You can share ideas on improving invitations, games, or stories. Y staff is always available to help your tribe develop good parents' meetings.

The following agenda and checklist should help you organize your parents' meetings.

Typical Parents' Meeting Agenda

8:00 p.m. Devotional thought

8:10 p.m. Review of agenda for this meeting

8:15 p.m. Consideration of items you desire to coordinate and plan (upcoming tribal meetings, special events, trips, etc.)

8:30 p.m. Special training and/or discussion of tribal problems

8:50 p.m. Any unfinished business

9:00 p.m. Scheduling of the next meeting and adjournment

Checklist for Meeting

- Call parents the night before to ensure attendance.
- Start on time.
- Give everyone a chance to contribute.
- Reach agreements on items.
- Make specific assignments.
- Set a date for the next parents' meeting.
- Serve refreshments during the meeting.
- Close on time.
- Distribute minutes of the meeting to all members.

To assist you in long-range planning, a group planning chart is included on the next two pages.

GROUP PLANNING CHART

Name of group or tribe _____

Number of adults _____ Number of children _____

What are our fixed activities for the year (e.g., meeting dates as planned at the fall parents' meeting, YMCA camp-outs, Pinewood Derby)?

_____   _____

_____   _____

_____   _____

_____   _____

_____   _____

What activities would we like to include (e.g., additional camp-outs, group outings)?

_____

_____

_____

_____

_____

_____

_____

_____

_____

_____

_____

_____

_____

Month	First Meeting	Second Meeting	Camp-Outs	Other Activities	Special Outings/ Camp-Outs
September					
October					
November					
December					
January					
February					
March					
April					
May					
June					
July					
August					

Suggested Parents' Leadership Roles

Offices held within each tribe provide shared leadership opportunities for personal development of both parents and children. Training opportunities for tribal chiefs are essential for effective tribal functioning. The roles found in many tribes include the Chief, Assistant Chief, Wampum Bearer, Tallykeeper, and Sachem.

- *Chief.* One of the parents is selected to see that there is continuity in meetings, conduct portions of the meetings, and act as the leader of the group. He or she presides at parents' meetings, delegates assignments, and checks to see that tasks are being done. He or she is the tribal contact person for the YMCA and represents the tribe at the monthly or semimonthly Longhouse/Nation meetings. (Some tribes change Chiefs every six months, but tribes should recognize the need for continuity and ongoing contact with the YMCA Director.)
- *Assistant Chief.* He or she assumes the duties of the Chief when the Chief is not able to attend meetings. He or she may accompany the Chief to Longhouse/Nation meetings and may be in training for the Chief's job.
- *Wampum Bearer.* This parent is responsible for the collection and safekeeping of the tribal wampum (dues) and has responsibility for collecting and forwarding to the YMCA monies for membership, camp-outs, and so forth.
- *Tallykeeper.* This parent takes care of attendance at tribal meetings. He or she might also be responsible for sending information on tribal activities to the YMCA and birthday cards to the tribal Braves/Princesses/Maidens on their birthdays.
- *Sachem.* The wise parent of the tribe—usually a former Chief—assumes this role. He or she reminds all members of the aims of the program, leads the tribe in many service projects, and helps to establish new tribes.

A tribe is free to create new or additional offices, and all parents should hold some office; however, offices should have specific tasks assigned to them. One word of caution: Avoid using names that have a religious meaning (Medicine Man or Woman) or demeaning implications among American Indian people. Office titles such as Craft Maker, Sign Maker, Council Judge, and the like are acceptable and have been adopted by some groups.

Tribal Property

Every tribe should make its own set of tribal property, which may include the following items:

- *Tribal drum.* The tribal drum is used to open and close each tribal meeting and represents the unity of the tribe.
- *Property box.* This box holds most of the tribal property, but should be small enough to be handled easily.
- *Totem pole.* One of the most important tribal properties, the pole is constructed of different sections made by each parent-child team.
- *Talking sticks or rocks.* During tribal meetings, the person holding the talking stick or rock is granted the right to speak. Talking sticks and rocks can be decorated with paint, feathers, beads, leather, or any other materials.
- *Council fire.* A "fire" made by nailing or screwing six to ten sticks together in the shape of a tepee, log cabin, or combination of both mounted on a plywood board, and placing a light bulb in the center to simulate a fire.
- *Coup stick.* These large decorated sticks are displayed outside the home to welcome tribal members. Each parent-child team can insert a feather when they arrive and remove it when they leave.
- *Tallykeeper's book.* A book constructed for the purpose of holding records of meetings and events. It may be decorated with various Indian designs.
- *Wampum or money pouch.* A leather container for holding tribal funds, often decorated with beads and feathers.

Tribal property belongs to the tribe and is made by tribal members. All materials should be purchased with tribal funds. The tribal properties are kept in the property box, which is taken by the next host after each meeting. Thus all property is kept intact and is readily available at the site of each successive meeting.

Each parent and child should share responsibility for making some of the tribal property.

Perhaps two families can work together to make the larger items. The important point is to make all properties as quickly as possible by including all parent-child teams in the fun and responsibility. Successful tribes complete these projects early, an achievement that helps knit the tribal members closely together. Moreover, the equipment adds color and meaning to meetings, increasing the satisfaction of all members.

Children's Responsibilities

Like parents, children have specific responsibilities in conducting the tribal meetings and maintaining the strength of the tribe. These responsibilities are paying dues, presenting scouting reports, and assuming some leadership functions.

Dues

In addition to the program fee charged by the YMCA, each tribe may collect tribal dues (wampum money) from the children for its own tribal use. The amount is set by the tribe and handled by the Wampum Bearer. Tribes use the money to pay for special treats, craft costs, gasoline on trips, and other items and events.

Each child should be prepared to tell other tribe members what he or she did to earn the wampum. This approach helps children learn the value of money and encourages them to do things for others.

Scouting Reports

The scouting report is an assignment given to the Little Braves/Princesses/Maidens by the Chief to be completed between meetings. By making a short report to the tribe, children develop poise and speaking ability, exercise their inquisitive and thoughtful natures, and practice responsible behavior. Scouting reports could include bringing in magazine pictures of certain scenes, activities, or cultures; making a list of insects found in the backyard; and the like. It's a good idea to recognize the children for their efforts in giving scouting reports.

Suggested Children's Leadership Roles

Children can learn leadership qualities by filling one or more of the suggested leadership roles in tribal meetings. These roles include the following:

- Young Chief. Usually the Chief's son or daughter assumes this role. He or she helps keep the children attentive, assists in the ceremonies, and reports tribal activities to the Nation or Longhouse news editor.
- Drum Beater. Usually the host child assumes this role. He or she is in charge of the tribal drum, calls everyone to council, and assists in ceremonies.
- Indian Runner. He or she keeps all headbands and tribal property in the property box and runs errands for the Chief.
- Wampum or Dues Collector. Usually the son or daughter of the Wampum Bearer assumes this role. He or she helps the Wampum Bearer to collect tribal dues and asks the young Braves/Princesses/Maidens whether they earned their money by service to family or community. In addition, this child finds out what activities parents took part in with their children in the past weeks.
- Roll Taker. The son or daughter of the Tallykeeper calls the roll using the tribal members' Indian names.

 # CONDUCTING TRIBAL MEETINGS

The outline shown here is a suggested guide for conducting a typical tribal meeting. It is followed by more detailed information on different parts of the meeting: tribal rituals, collection of wampum, scouting reports, Chief's talks, and the Tallykeeper's reports. The final section offers some hints for running interesting meetings.

7:00 p.m.   Chief calls meeting to order by asking one of the children to beat on the tribal drum once for each parent-child team present. Talking should stop. Chief leads prayer or opening ceremony and flag salute (if flag is available).

7:10 p.m.   Tallykeeper takes roll (and may also read minutes of last meeting). Wampum Bearer collects tribal dues; each Little Brave/ Princess/Maiden explains how he or she obtained wampum. Wampum bag is passed around.

7:15 p.m.   Chief asks for scouting reports. Use of the talking stick is recommended as each child presents a scouting report. (Chief's talk may follow.)

7:25 p.m.   Chief announces any upcoming intertribal events, YMCA news, and so forth. Plans are reviewed for next meeting, using the "Group Planning Chart" on page 17 of this manual.

7:35 p.m.   Tribe makes a craft or plays a game.

7:50 p.m.   Host serves light refreshments.

8:00 p.m.   Tribal member tells a story and/or tribe sings songs.

8:20 p.m.   Chief leads closing ritual and/or prayer.

8:25 p.m.   Tribe heads for home.

Tribal Rituals

Opening and closing rituals add a great deal to your meetings. Rituals are exciting to children of this age. They should be simple, brief, and dignified. You can vary procedures and content if the additions make the ceremony more meaningful to your tribe. In the first few meetings, the parts of the rituals can be read, but they should be memorized as soon as possible.

Do not underestimate the importance of rituals. A tribal ceremony should be used at every tribal meeting, and it should be performed consistently from meeting to meeting.

Opening Rituals

All meetings begin on time with the beating of the drum. A drum should be one of the first tribal craft projects, as it adds a great deal to the meetings. Parents and children form a double circle, with the children standing in the inner circle in front of their own parents. When all are quiet, the ceremony is conducted with dignity and meaning. The beginning of each meeting can follow a ritual format as shown in the following outlines. Where multiple choices are offered (such as Braves/Princesses/ Maidens), use only the one appropriate for your group.

Outline 1

Drum Beater (the host child) gives the drum twelve beats (or one for each parent-child team present).

CHIEF: (Raising hands and eyes to the Great Spirit) *Great Spirit, as we gather around this council fire, dwell among us and guide us. Give us wisdom and understanding. In this, the month of the _____ moon* (see Indian pictographs in the "Indian Theme" section for names of moons), *we are grateful for _____* (something simple that the children will understand: the beautiful weather; the large attendance; the beautiful outing we just had), *O Great Spirit, hear our words.*

OR

CHIEF: *Let us give thanks for our loved ones, for the beauty of the Earth, and for the Creator's blessings.*

OR

CHIEF: *O God, as we gather for this council, be with us and guide us. Grant us wisdom and understanding, that we may do those things that are pleasing to you. We thank you for _____.*

Drum Beater beats drum twice.

CHIEF: *What is the slogan of Y-Indian Guides/ Princesses/Maidens/Braves?*

ALL: *The slogan is "Pals Forever"/"Friends Always."*

CHIEF: *Drum Beater, what is a Y-Indian Brave/ Princess/Maiden?*

DRUM BEATER: *A boy/girl with a dad/mom like mine.*

CHIEF: *And your office, what does it mean?*

DRUM BEATER: *The beating of the drum calls the tribe together and tells its members to come to order.*

CHIEF: *Indian Runner, what are the duties and meaning of your office?*

INDIAN RUNNER: *I stand guard over the tribal property.*

CHIEF: *What is the pledge of all Y-Indian Braves/ Princesses/Maidens?*

ALL: *Our daily pledge is "We, father/mother and son/daughter, through friendly service to each other, to our family, to this tribe, to our community, seek a world pleasing to the eye of the Great Spirit."*

CHIEF: *This council is now open. Sit.* (Each parent takes a seat on the floor, with the child in front.)

CHIEF: *Tallykeeper, read the Birch Bark Scroll.*

TALLYKEEPER: (Reads the minutes of the last meeting.)

CHIEF: *Tallykeeper, will you take the roll while the Wampum Bearer collects the dues and calls for scouting reports?*

The children pay their dues, tell how they obtained the money, and report on any special thing that occurred during the time between meetings. Each child should have a turn to speak and should be encouraged to participate.

TALLYKEEPER: *Chief, the roll has been called.*

WAMPUM BEARER: *Chief, the dues are collected, and the scouting reports received.*

Outline 2

CHIEF: *Drum Beater, beat the drum to call the tribe to order.*

Drum Beater strikes twelve beats on the drum slowly.

CHIEF: *All stand for the Pledge of Allegiance.*

ALL: (Say the Pledge of Allegiance.)

CHIEF: *Young Braves/Princesses/Maidens, what is a Y-Indian Brave/Princess/Maiden?*

CHILDREN: *A boy/girl with a dad/mom like mine.*

CHIEF: *What is the purpose of the Y-Indian Guides/Princesses/Maidens/Braves?*

ALL: *To foster the understanding and companionship between father and son/father and daughter/mother and daughter/mother and son.*

CHIEF: *What is the slogan of the Y-Indian Guides/Princesses/Maidens/Braves?*

ALL: *"Pals Forever"/"Friends Always."* (Chief then leads all in repeating aims of their program.)

CHIEF: *Drum Beater, what are the duties of your office?*

DRUM BEATER: *The duties of the Drum Beater are to beat the drum to call the meeting to order.*

CHIEF: *Indian Runner, what are the duties of your office?*

INDIAN RUNNER: *My duties are to answer all calls and run errands for the tribe.*

CHIEF: *Tallykeeper, what are the duties of your office?*

TALLYKEEPER: *The duties of the Tallykeeper shall be to record all events of each meeting of the _____ tribe and give a copy of the record to the Chief at the following meeting.*

CHIEF: *Tallykeeper, read the record from the last meeting.*

TALLYKEEPER: (Reads the minutes of the last meeting.)

CHIEF: *Wampum Bearer, what are the duties of your office?*

WAMPUM BEARER: *The duties of the Wampum Bearer are to collect the dues and handle the finances of our tribe.*

CHIEF: *Tallykeeper, call the roll while the Wampum Bearer collects the dues.*

The Tallykeeper now calls the children one at a time, by their Indian names. As the child's name is called, he or she stands up and goes to the Wampum Bearer. The Wampum Bearer asks the child how the money was obtained. The child replies.

TALLYKEEPER: *Chief, the roll is called.*

WAMPUM BEARER: *Chief, the dues have been collected.*

Closing Rituals

Each meeting should close with a short, simple ritual. This joins the tribe together once more before leaving and provides a suitable ending to the meeting. The following are some examples.

And now (*index finger pointing to the ground*), may the Great Spirit (*all fingers circling up, imitating smoke*) of all good spirits (*arms outstretched*) be with (*arms coming in close*) you (*index finger pointing across circle*), now (*all fingers pointing down*) and forever more (*action of shooting bow and arrow*).

May the Great Spirit (*sign of "V" with right hand up and forward from shoulder*) look down upon us (*the "V" fingers bent forward and down and wrist bent forward, so that the V fingers "look* down") while we are absent (*two index fingers held before body, about a foot apart, then drawn together*) for a little while (*index fingers drawn apart, the left forward, the right backwards, for about a six-inch space*).

During each of the following prayers, raise your arms above your head at the beginning of the prayer and slowly lower them during the prayer:

Great Spirit of the Universe, guide us until we meet again.

O Great Spirit, watch over us during the passing moon, hear our voices and guide our thoughts.

O Chief of Gods, aid us in our tribe, watch over our tepees, and protect our Braves/Princesses/Maidens.

Great Spirit, hear our voices asking for guidance and direction from the winds; we will watch the setting sun as a sign of your power.

One by one, the children remove their own and their parents' council feathers from the tribal coup stick to indicate that the tribal council is over and that the members are leaving.

Other Ceremonies

Certain special ceremonies should be a part of your program as well: the induction of new members and tribes, the induction of new officers, and the passing of the headdress from the old Chief to the new one. Suggested formats for some of these ceremonies will be described in the forthcoming revision of the *Leaders Manual*. Make these ceremonies impressive and see how they add spark to your program.

Collection of Wampum

The collection of wampum can be one of the most effective portions of the tribal meeting for both children and parents. It gives the children a chance to learn about the value of money, to gain confidence in speaking before the group, to be inspired to do things for others, and to listen while other children report. It presents parents with an opportunity to ob-

serve their own children's poise and thinking processes as they speak and to learn how all of the children obtain the money for dues.

There should be a definite ceremonial flavor to this procedure. The Wampum Bearer should rise and display the contents of the wampum bag for all to see while proudly announcing how much is in the bag. The Wampum Collector then stands before each child and receives his or her wampum and the story of how it was obtained.

The Council Judge stands erect near the Chief. When all wampum is collected and all reports are in, that person says, "O Chief, I have heard the Braves/Princesses/Maidens of the mighty (*tribal name*) Y-Indian Guides/Princesses/Maidens/Braves tribe report the ways they have received their wampum, and I find those ways helpful to all."

The Chief then asks the Wampum Collector to deliver the wampum to the Wampum Bearer, who ceremoniously puts it into the tribal wampum bag.

A variation would be to have one of the parents tell how he or she earns wampum at work each day. Parents could bring examples and/or pictures of their work.

The Wampum Bearer and Collector will want to make a wampum pouch or bag. It can be made inexpensively from rawhide or leather or calfskin (with hair still on) in a number of simple ways. Instructions for creating a wampum pouch can be found in the "Tribal Property" section.

Presentation of Scouting Reports

The scouting reports are an important part of the tribal meeting. Children learn a great deal from presenting a report of something they did, heard, or saw since the last meeting. If the report is about something they did with their parents, so much the better. Children may need to be prompted at first to get started. Talk over the report with your son or daughter before the meeting to encourage him or her to speak.

Watch for subjects that make good scouting reports and point them out to your child. The small and unusual things in nature make the best reports. Encourage your child to ask questions about life, nature, work, mechanical devices, and the like, and then look up the answer with him or her for the report. Perhaps the best kind of report is a parent-child experience, whether a craft, a hike, or even a movie together.

These reports accomplish three important goals:

- Develop poise and speaking ability in a child and give him or her a sense of adding to the value of the meeting.
- Help the child to see what he or she is looking at, that is, to look more closely at nature, to view the very small and the very large, and to muse about what he or she has seen.
- Encourage parents to do more with their children.

The Chief in his or her talk can direct the children's attention to a special subject to help them make a report at the next meeting. Some possible topics are listed here:

Birds	Clouds
Athletics	Snakes
Growth	Favorite Indian
Fish	Rocks
Dogs	Seeds
Hobbies	Sign language
Stars	History of the tribal name
Flowers	
Trips	Ocean
What they want to be	Feathers
Trees	Family

Recognize the children for their efforts in making scouting reports by giving them a bead or feather as a form of encouragement.

Chief's Talks

Immediately following the opening ceremony, the Chief may say a few words to the tribe, giving Indian information, telling of a great Indian or tribe, reminding the tribe of its ideals, or speaking of the Great Spirit or wonders of nature. This provides an opportunity to teach values to sons and daughters. The talk should not be long and should be determined by the children's attention span. If they get restless,

bring the talk to a close. The following are examples of ideas to include in the Chief's talks:

- Respect for the family, including things that parents and children can do at home
- Tribal problems: for example, use an Aesop's fable to make a point
- An animal story that encourages good conduct or builds interest in the out-of-doors
- The meaning of the tribal headband and the importance of tribal aims
- An explanation of Indian sign language or sign writing
- The wonderful things the tribe has done that it can be proud of
- Interesting facts and stories from magazines
- An explanation of the seasons in terms of Indians and hunters or gatherers
- An invitation for parents and children to talk over their misunderstandings together

Simple examples from nature can make children think about what they see. These are some examples:

- Did you know that ants carry over 100 times their own weight? They need this strength in order to build their homes. If we had the same strength, we could carry over seven tons. Do we need this kind of strength?
- Did you know that one of the slowest, dumbest animals in the forest is the porcupine? In addition, it doesn't have good eyes or claws. But it's protected by quills from enemies. Why?
- Have you ever noticed a sea anemone? It is a little animal that looks like a piece of shell or rock in the shallow pools by the ocean. If you touch it, it closes and looks just like the bottom of the pool. Why is it protected?
- Have you ever thought about how a grasshopper is like Superman? It has huge legs and big muscles to jump great heights. If we could jump as high as a grasshopper can, we could jump over the Empire State Building in a single bound.
- Have you ever caught a lizard by its tail and then had the tail come off in your hand? Lizards can drop their tails and grow new ones. Why do they have this special trick?
- Have you heard about the snowshoe rabbit? It changes color twice a year. In the sum-

mer it's brown, but when winter comes it turns snow-white. Why?

- Did you know that there is a spinning wheel attached to spiders? The spider can spin its own web, creating the most delicate designs. Why does it need this spinning wheel?

Tallykeeper's Report

The Tallykeeper has a real job to do in writing up the minutes of the previous tribal meeting in an imaginative way. The Tallykeeper and son or daughter should work on the minutes together, using Indian terms and symbols where possible and bringing in enough humor to interest the other children.

Verbal reports made at meetings should be kept brief. More detailed written reports can be prepared for the tribal history book. The following is a sample report:

Tallykeeper's Report

Council fire at the wigwam of Strong Bow and Fleet Arrow on the Seventh Sun of the Rose Moon. All members were called to council by papoose-sized bow and arrow.

Chief Moose Hoof gave war whoop when all members entered wigwam on time. Little Deer beat the drum, and Coyote led chants, but he sounded like a sick coyote. All members were good on ritual . . . they knew parts as a squirrel knows an acorn.

Chief Moose Hoof told tribe about weeds and how they hold tightly to the ground when pulled up. The Great Spirit made strong roots for them so that they might grow tall and strong before they travel to the Happy Hunting Ground. The Great Spirit loves and protects all—even weeds.

Tallykeeper found all braves present at council fire.

Wampum Collector gathered wampum and heard good reports on how wampum was gained. Wampum Bearer found eight frog skins (dollars) and seventy-two pebbles (cents) in wampum pouch.

War Chief Badger Eye said it was time for big tribal move to shores of Gitchee Gumie for fishing. A show of feathers indicated we would take trip in twelve suns to Redondo Village Canoe Landing.

Scouting report showed wide-open eyes and listening ears on part of all members. Brave Little Tepee was granted "Brave of the Month" for scouting out fossil rock in Palos Verdes hunting ground.

Assistant Chief Bald Eagle gave many praises to the members who went to the House of the Great Spirit, saved wampum, made a project, and helped brothers and sisters at the Tuba City Reservation.

Braves Big and Little Bear showed the tribe how to make an arm bussle out of papoose feathers and hide from unlucky cow. Little Bear gave out materials for braves to make arm bussles before next council.

Chief Moose Hoof told great tale of faraway Indian tribe of Incas who worshiped the Sun because they thought the Great Spirit was the Boss of the Sun.

Braves had chocolate corn bread and 7-Up from hands of Kau Strong Bow.

Braves played "Steal the Scalp," but little braves said they could not find scalp on Bald Eagle's head.

Chief Moose Hoof closed council meeting with Omaha Tribal Prayer.

Good Practices for Interesting Meetings

The Chief and tribal officers should keep effective group practices in mind in their planning and appraisal of tribal development. Remember that the basic purpose of Y-Indian Guide Programs is to increase the number of things parents and children can enjoy doing together during the time when children think their parents are the greatest. Thus it is important that the tribal meeting be interesting to the young children and that they have ample opportunity to participate. The meetings must be oriented toward the children, not the parents.

Use the following suggestions as a guide for devising interesting meetings:

- Be concerned about all group members, the shy as well as the outgoing.
- Start meetings on time; close them on time. Opening ceremonies should not spill over into program time.
- Aim the ceremonial parts of the meeting at the children. They should do most of the talking during the meetings; it should be fun for them.

- Focus program activities on the interests and capabilities of the children. Be alert to their needs.
- Plan all phases of the tribal meeting carefully; contact families with special responsibilities in advance. It is the Chief's job to see that the Chief's talk, reports, stories, games, and so on are chosen beforehand.
- Encourage all; share praise where it is deserved. Recognize the progress of all Braves/Princesses/Maidens.
- Allow for a great deal of fun at tribal meetings; support joint participation by fathers/mothers and sons/daughters.
- Pass responsibility around: Know the individual tribal members' interests and experiences. Assign tasks carefully.
- Be wary of parents' talking too much in tribal meetings; use parents' meetings regularly to handle most business.
- Facilitate team discussion and decision making on matters of behavior, program development, and policy for the tribe.
- Be warm, supportive, understanding, and flexible. Be more concerned about the feelings and attitudes of tribal members than with the accuracy of tribal ceremonies or procedures.

Use the following list to troubleshoot problems with your meetings.

If this is happening in your Indian tribe	*Do this*
Can't get meetings started on time.	Have late parents and children sit on the floor.
Meetings run too late.	Set alarm clock to ring at end of meeting ceremony and at end of program time.
Parents talk too much.	Have one parent keep a record of times each parent speaks and discuss the problem at the next parents' meeting.
Children play while parents watch.	Plan games that call for parents and children to compete on the same team.
Parents talk business during meeting.	Chief stops this by referring matter to the next parents' meeting.
Children are inattentive during meeting, talking and giggling, or running around.	If the meeting is interesting to the children, they'll pay attention because they want to. Give the children things to do. Make the meetings fun.

Inappropriate behavior by children at meetings.

Check meeting and programs for level of children's interest. Decide what positive behaviors are desired and establish them through activities and rewards.

STARTING A TRIBE

If you are part of a group that is just entering one of the Y-Indian Guide Programs, this section will give you some vital information. The first part consists of steps to follow in establishing your tribe. The second part is a discussion of the selection of individual and tribal Indian names, and it includes a list of possible names from which to choose.

Initial Steps

Here is a list of steps for starting a new tribe. It may be of help to you and the other parent-child teams in your tribe. The first parents' meeting should take place as soon after the YMCA orientation meeting as possible. Schedule the first tribal meeting as soon as possible after the first parents' meeting.

First Parents' Meeting

- Select meeting night, set up dates of tribal meetings for next four months, and fill out activity chart for at least the next four months.
- Decide on wampum and amount and bring to the first tribal meeting.
- Choose tribal officers/roles.
- Decide on necessary tribal property; make assignments for projects that should be brought to first tribal meeting.

First Tribal Meeting

- Have each parent-child team pick out Indian names for themselves before the first tribal meeting.
- Introduce all tribal members by their new names.

Second Tribal Meeting

- Select Indian tribal name (check with Y office so as not to duplicate a tribal name already in use).

- Forward the list of tribal members on the official roster to the Y office along with completed registration forms and fees.

Induction Ceremony

- Date for official induction ceremony is set by the YMCA.

Indian Names

American Indians name their children for some event in the child's life, for an outstanding character trait, or for a spirit that they hope will guide the child. You can do the same, using either the English or Indian word. This section contains suggested Indian names or their English equivalents for parents, children, and new tribes.

Indian Names for Parents and Children

The selection of a name for parent and child should be done with the same respect and ceremony that is practiced by the American Indian. The name should reflect honor, and it should be carried with honor by the bearer.

The American Indians grant names to their children in the following ways, which your tribe can consider in selecting names that have meaning for each specific person.

- The elders' vision of what the child may turn out to be (i.e., a guide for his or her future, such as Silver Bird, Peacemaker, or Straight Arrow).
- Something that stood out in the parents' minds on the day the child was born (Bright Star, Snow Rabbit, Sleeping Bear).
- The hope of the parent or child for his or her future (Strong Heart, Steady Wind, Brave Wolf, Wise Owl).
- The traits of the parent or child (Great Thunder, Tall Cedar, Keen Eyes, Quiet Squirrel).
- An experience of great meaning to the family (Clear Water, Running Deer, Red Sky).

Some suggested English names:

Bright Star	Rising Sun
Cornplanter	Running Antelope
Flying Cloud	Running Rabbit
Great Star	Setting Sun
Looking Glass	Shooting Star
Medicine Crow	Silver Fox
Morning Cloud	Sky Woman
Peacemaker	Swift Cloud
Red Bird	Talking Rock
Red Cloud	White Antelope
Red Feather	White Bird
Red Fox	Young Fox

Children who wish to use authentic Indian names may find suggestions in the following list of names and their English translations:

Anang	Star
Anekus	Squirrel
Anoki	Actor
Apekatos	Antelope
Ayita	Worker
Apelachi	A Helper
Bebe-ji	Wild Horse
Bisanabi	The Silent One
Bineshi	Bird Sharp
Bebe-mak	Dark Horse
Bodaway	(He) Makes Fire
Chabadwed	Camp Cook
Chimalus	Bluebird
Chissakid	Juggler
Chule	Pine Tree
Monoway	Moving Voice
Namid	Dancer
Nas-waw-kee	Feathered Arrow
Nibaw	I Stand Up
Nina-bo-jou	Sun God
Nodin	Wind
Nokisan	Wonder Cook
On-jima	Strong Hand
Osohada	White Cedar
Panossim	Water Dog or Sea Dog
Sa-que-sippi	River of Mystery

Sheboygo	Writer
Skajuna	Eagle

When the Indian names are determined, a simple family ceremony can be done in which the child bestows the parent's Indian name and the parent bestows the child's Indian name.

Indian Tribal Names

In choosing your tribal name, remember that the careful search for an interesting name will not only be educational, but will result in a selection your tribe will be proud to bear. Some groups prefer a name from the tribes that lived in their areas. Some pick a name because the tribe had particularly admirable qualities or because it's a fascinating or amusing name. Some create a tribal name by using the Indian word for a quality they wish to accentuate in their activities. A check with the Longhouse will avoid duplication along with gaining approval of your choice.

To start you thinking, here are a few tribal names and their meanings:

Mohawks	People of the Flint
Oneidas	People of the Upright Stone
Senecas	People of the Great Mountains
Cayugas	People of the Mucklands
Onondagas	Hill People
Tuscaroras	Wearers of Shirts

Listed below are the more familiar authentic tribal names taken from a list based on ten cultural areas of the Indian tribes of the United States:

California Indians

Achomawi	Kern River	Salinan
Algonquian	Klamath	Serrano
Athapaskan	Koso	Shasta
Atsugewi	Luiseño	Shoshone
Cahuilla	Lutuami	Tolowa
Chemehuevi	Maidu	Wailaki
Chumash	Miwok	Wappo
Diegueño	Modoc	Washo
Fernandeño	Mohave	Wintu
Gabrielino	Mono	Wiyot
Halchidoma	Nicoleño	Yana
Hokan	Paiute	Yokuts

Island Chumash	Penutian	Yuki
Juaneño	Pit River	Yuma
Kamia	Playanos	Yurok
Karok	Pomo	
Kawaiisu	Purisimeño	

Southwest Indians (Arizona and New Mexico)

Anasazi	Jicarilla Apache	Tiwas
Apache	Keresans	Towa
Carrizo	Maricopa	Walapai
Chemehuevi	Mohave	Yagui
Cocopa	Navajo	Yavapai
Havasupai	Paiute	Yumans
Hopi	Papago	Zuni
Hualapais	Pima	
Isleta Pueblo	Tewas	

Lower Plateau Indians (Colorado, Nevada, and Utah)

Apache	Kaibab	Uncompahgre
Arapahoe	Kiowa	Ute
Bannock	Monache	Washo
Capote	Navajo	Weeminuche
Cheyenne	Paiute	Yampa
Comanche	Paviotso	
Goshute	Shoshone	

Gulf Coast Indians (Florida, Alabama, Mississippi, Louisiana, and Texas)

Apache	Chitimacha	Seminole
Apalachee	Choctaw	Tawakoni
Apalachicola	Comanche	Timucua
Atakapa	Coushatta	Tonkawa
Biloxi	Creeks	Tunica
Caddo	Houma	Yuchi
Calusa	Muskhogee	
Chickasaw	Natchez	

Northwest Indians (Washington, Oregon, and Idaho)

Bannock	Lummi	Salish
Cayuse	Makah	Sanpoil
Chinook	Nez Percé	Shoshone
Colville	Nootka	Spokan
Duwamish	Paiute	Takelma
Kalispel	Palouse	Umatilla
Kiturahan	Penutian	Wallawalla
Klamath	Quinault	Yakima
Kutenai	Quileute	

Indians of Montana and Wyoming

Arapahoe	Chippewa	Salish
Assiniboin	Cree	Shoshone
Bannock	Crow	Sioux
Blackfeet	Gros Ventres	Ute
Cheyenne	Nez Percé	

Plains and Prairie Indians (North and South Dakota, Nebraska, Kansas, Oklahoma, Iowa, Missouri, and Arkansas)

Arapahoe	Foxes	Osage
Arikara	Hidatsa	Oto
Assiniboin	Iowa	Pawnee
Cherokee	Kansa	Ponca
Cheyenne	Kiowa	Quapaw
Chickasaw	Mandan	Seminole
Chippewa	Missouri	Seneca
Choctaw	Moingwena	Shawnee
Comanche	Okmulgee	Sioux
Creeks	Omaha	Wichita

Great Lakes Indians (Minnesota, Michigan, Ohio, Illinois, Indiana, and Wisconsin)

Chippewa	Kickapoo	Potawatomi
Delaware	Mascouten	Sauk
Erie	Menominee	Shawnee
Foxes	Miami	Sioux
Huron	Mohegan	Winnebago
Illinois	Ojibwa	
Iroquois	Ottawa	

Northeastern Woodland Indians (Virginia, Kentucky, and All New England States)

Abenaki	Montauk	Penacook
Delaware	Nanticoke	Pequot
Iroquois	Narragansett	Powhatan
Massachusett	Maliseet-Passamaquoddy	Susquehannock
Mohegan	Penobscot	
Moneton		

Southeastern Woodland Indians (Tennessee, North and South Carolina, and Georgia)

Alabama	Chickahominy	Powhatan
Apalachee	Chickasaw	Shawnee
Atakapa	Croatan	Tunica
Biloxi	Mattapony	Tuscarora
Catawba	Natchez	Waco
Cherokee	Pamlico	Yuchi

PROGRAM EVALUATION

The evaluation sheet found on the next page can be used by program leaders who visit tribes (see *Leaders Manual*) or by tribal leaders to evaluate themselves and set goals for the coming months. Follow these steps in its use:

1. Agree upon a single, one-hour discussion period for parents alone.
2. Have each parent read all questions and decide upon three or four of the most important ones.
3. Tally the top three priority questions of each parent and determine the top five for follow-up.
4. Addressing one question at a time
   a. identify how well the tribe is doing in this area,
   b. agree on one or two steps for improvement, and
   c. assign responsibilities to parents.
5. Seek the help of others in Steps 2 through 4. Involve the Longhouse officer, local schoolteachers or ministers, and/or the YMCA staff.

Y-Indian Guide Programs Evaluation Sheet

How Important as a Goal?					How Well Achieved in Tribal Program?			
Great	Some	Slight	None		Poorly	Needs Improve-ment	Satis-factorily	Very Well
				1. Does your tribe get parents and children to spend more time to-gether, in an increasing variety of activities, outside of tribal meetings?				
				2. Do the parents look forward to be-ing with each other in the meetings and activities?				
				3. Do the parents relax and enjoy the time with their children in tribal meetings and activities, with the parents doing a minimum of com-peting through their children?				
				4. Do parents and children talk together more—understand and like each other more—as a result of the tribe?				
				5. Are the other family members in-cluded in some activities in such a way that they are glad the parent and child belong to the tribe?				
				6. Are parents and children proud of the tribe and what it accomplishes?				
				7. Do children get opportunities and encouragement to express them-selves—show what they can do, say what they think of the tribe activi-ties, carry out officer duties?				
				8. Do the parents sometimes swap ideas with each other about their children?				
				9. Do parents and children sometimes have experiences in tribal activities that make them aware of spiritual things—God and higher ideals?				
				10. Do all members feel wanted, needed, important in the tribe?				
				11. Is the responsibility for operation of the tribe shared by all the parents?				
				12. Do the children understand and think about the Y-Indian Guide Pro-gram's aims?				
				13. Do the parents teach their children new skills?				
				14. Do the kind of activities and the way the tribe operates give children opportunities to see their parents act as adults?				
				15. Do the parents contribute leader-ship to organize and strengthen other tribes?				
				16. Do the parents feel responsible for helping all the children?				
				17. Do the members feel a part of the Y as a whole and accept its aims?				

Program Planning

This section is designed to help you and the other parents in your tribe develop a satisfying program of tribal activities for your group. You'll want to keep in mind that parent-child interaction is the focus of the Y-Indian Guide Programs and that each program's six aims can provide a structure for your program. Later in this section the advantages and disadvantages of prepared versus original program activities are discussed, and there is a list of suggested objectives for tribal programs. As the children change and grow, you will want to change the program; to that end, ideas for projects, recreation, invitations, sports and games, trips, and ceremonies are included. Some tribes may want to dedicate part of their time to parent education, and all tribes should consider carefully whether they want to use award systems as part of their program.

THE PARENT-CHILD FOCUS

Program projects provide a variety of opportunities for you and your children to develop understanding, affection, and mutual respect. Shared experiences, such as working on crafts together, playing games and doing stunts, walking and talking, exchanging ideas, telling stories, and carrying out service projects, are fundamental in building healthy parent-child relationships through Y-Indian Guide Programs. Program projects should be chosen to correlate with the age, ability, and experience of the children and to encourage parent-child participation.

Y-Indian Guide Program experiences will enable you to appreciate your children's individual differences. As you observe your children interacting with others, you will begin to recognize the particular developmental needs of your own daughters or sons. In turn, your children will gain a new understanding of you and other adults from seeing parents have fun together and plan for others. Children are very proud of the special time and attention that parents give them in Y-Indian Guide Programs. They also learn how to get along with other children, and they seem to increase their ability to function within their own families. The Y-Indian Guide Programs offer opportunities for both parents and children to gain new information and insights about their neighborhood, other families, and the larger community.

Program activities and experiences will afford you the chance to share your affection with your children. It will also allow you to help your sons and daughters learn new social skills and master physical challenges. By helping children function effectively in a group, you will support their personal growth among their peers. In addition, you can make a significant contribution to your children's spiritual lives by helping them gain a deeper reverence for God and for basic spiritual values.

THE SIX AIMS

Each program's aims can be focal points for physical, mental, social, and spiritual learning opportunities and skills development. Such structured planning ensures variety and continuity of experience. You and your children can examine the meaning of each aim together through activities and situations designed to help children grow and mature. You can provide a wide range of quality programming through thoughtful appraisal, adaptation, and creative planning.

easier to be fully involved. You can derive much fulfillment from creating your own programs or adapting prepared ones to your own needs.

PROGRAM SPONTANEITY

Every beginning leader looks avidly for tried-and-true programs that can be followed automatically. This is especially true of new adult Y-Indian Guide Program members, who feels shaky at the beginning of the tribe's life about what to do with this vibrant group of energetic children. To help you get started, many concrete program aids appear in this manual. Such prepared programs can also help educate all tribe members about Indian culture, which is the brick-and-mortar background of this program.

The process of getting organized and learning about the program itself is part of the program at the beginning. All the facets of good programs are inherent in this initial activity— involvement, purpose, creative initiative, group formation, interpersonal interaction and stimulation, socialization, friendship formation, mutual support, and learning about the material that is discussed.

Beyond this, each group itself is a rich program resource for developing its own program ideas. Each parent and child comes to the group endowed with personal interests and skills. Each neighborhood or community has a special character that contributes to the ideas and activities that the group develops. Cooperative efforts utilizing the YMCA staff, local church and school personnel, and community resources can also lead to creative, happy, and worthwhile program experiences for parents and children.

No manual of program ideas can top the quality of programs spontaneously produced out of the natural interests and needs of a specific group. When your group develops activities that are your own, you will find it easier to identify with the activity; it also will be

OBJECTIVES FOR TRIBAL PROGRAMS

As you seek to develop a balanced and meaningful Y-Indian Guide Program experience, focus on objectives in the following areas to support the children's growth: understanding of family life, skills development, education for life enrichment, group organization and functioning, community awareness, and spiritual growth.

1. Understanding family life
   a. The adult's role as a mother or father
   b. The distinction between parent and child roles
   c. The fostering of significant communication and relationships among all members of the family
   d. The development of responsibility and mutual concern
2. Skills development
   a. Health and physical fitness
      (1) Motor skills
      (2) Hand-eye coordination
      (3) Physical fitness
   b. Mental skills
      (1) Support in reading and verbalization
      (2) Creative expression
      (3) Development of self-direction
   c. Social skills
      (1) Relating to others
      (2) Expressing concern and having respect for others
      (3) Developing a sense of humor and the ability to listen
3. Education for life enrichment
   a. Being exposed to new ideas and concepts

b. Understanding and appreciating American Indian culture

c. Learning by doing—direct participation and observation

d. Exploring vocations

e. Learning about nature and the interdependence of all life

4. Group organization and functioning

a. Working with others as part of a group

b. Providing leadership

c. Assuming responsibility voluntarily

d. Carrying out tasks for the benefit of all

5. Community awareness

a. Visiting new and old community institutions

b. Meeting community leaders

c. Recognizing the needs of others and providing service

6. Spiritual growth

a. Developing warm, pleasant parent and child relationships

b. Pursuing outdoor nature activities

c. Participating in sincere, well-prepared, worshipful devotional experiences

PROGRAM PROGRESSION

Because children develop new skills and capabilities as they grow, they can participate in progressively more complex experiences and activities as they move from the first to the third year of the Y-Indian Guide Programs. The following outlines describe how activities can be changed over time. Although this information will be most directly applicable to tribes composed of children of similar ages, all adults should be aware of the changes that take place in children between the ages of five and nine.

It is essential to take the time to plan for new experiences that build on children's initial activities and that challenge them to learn new responsibilities. These new activities should also satisfy the different interests and talents of the parents. Plan wisely. Beware of repeating experiences or activities that worked well once—children change quickly.

Program for the First Year (Kindergarten and First Grade)

Projects

During this first year the young Braves/Princesses/Maidens will have limited skills and dexterity. Crafts should be kept simple; you will need to help out a great deal. It is important for you to get to know each other, to tap each other's resources, and to understand the potential of the program. Activities should be related to the abilities of the five- to six-year-old.

Major emphasis should be placed upon making tribal property, such as the tribal drum, totem pole, rattles, and standards. Individual projects should include drawing and painting for decoration and the making of headbands, vests, or household aids.

Recreation

Play is a very important means for children's social and personal development. Games, songs, stories, and other recreational activities should help the children grow and hold their interest. Children need to learn appreciation of rules and the rights of others, and play is the primary arena for this learning. Outdoor hiking, trips, and family picnics are constructive activities.

Invitations

Invitations are very appropriate as a project and program activity. Children should be encouraged to express themselves through simple designs and colorful decorations.

Sports and Games

This is not the time for promoting organized games such as baseball, basketball, and football. Children of this age need to run, jump, and skip. They need help in riding a bicycle and in rollerskating. Focus on informal social recreation games with limited skill requirements.

Trips

Trips should expose children to new experiences and foster new ideas. Destinations should include visits to the zoo, aquarium, dairy, farm, museum, and park. Technical explanations should be kept to a minimum. Learning about animals from firsthand experience is very exciting and attractive.

Ceremonies

Acquiring a feeling for special occasions is an important learning experience. During the first year you probably should adhere closely to the tribal council ceremonies outlined in this manual. Set an example for the children by establishing a climate of dignity and joy in the meetings.

First Year

- Members get acquainted and lay the foundation.
- Parents lead the group.
- Children have short attention spans and limited skills.
- Children explore and test relationships.
- The program is oriented toward the individual.

Program for the Second Year (Second Grade)

Projects

The seven-year-old child should be more prepared for actual Indian-type crafts and lore. Projects might include armbands, Indian belts, vests, imitation campfires, new headbands, and anklets. It is important that all projects be done by both parent and child. What young Braves/Princesses/Maidens do, you should do.

Recreation

Recreation at meetings should start to change. Teach Indian sign language, along with dances and stories. Let the children tell stories as well. Relay games and fun stunts are appropriate to this age group.

Invitations

Continue having the children make invitations as a project. They should be encouraged to take a more active part in planning and working than they might have in the first year.

Sports and Games

Some seven-year-olds are ready for active organized sports; others are not. Play games such as four-square and dodgeball, but don't make the rules too complicated. Don't focus strongly on learning skills. Allow the children to have fun; they'll start to pick up skills automatically. Swimming is an excellent activity for parents and children to share.

Trips

Children this age usually are not ready for long or involved trips. Take them to places where they can keep moving about. Their attention span is short. After a trip, recount what happened that was new or of special interest.

Ceremonies

Change any part of the program that no longer fits a need or interest. Add new ideas and discard the routine things that no longer serve a purpose. Appoint children to participate in specific roles.

Special Events

Family picnics or outings, parent-and-child banquets, fishing derbies, kite-flying events, and camp-outs are wonderful social-learning settings and communication experiences for both second- and third-year tribes.

Second Year

- Members build on new parent-child relationships.
- Children share in program responsibility.
- Children develop their basic motor skills.
- The group does more community exploration and takes more trips.
- The program is oriented toward nurturing concern for others.

Program for Third Year (Third and Fourth Grades)

Projects

Most children eight to nine years of age can do a fine job at handicrafts. It is important to keep the young Braves/Princesses/Maidens interested by providing a good program. Projects to consider are whittling, woodburning, basket weaving, soap carving, and making Indian costumes, beadwork, gourd rattles, pottery, soft metal crafts, and birdhouses. Parents should be strategic aides and consultants for this age group.

Recreation

Set some meetings aside just for crafts. Skip longer ceremonies and business meetings; try to accomplish a project during the evening. Allow the children to assume some leadership roles by having them tell stories or lead the tribe in songs. Continue encouraging and supporting the children with lots of praise.

It is important to make crafts in homes with adequate facilities. Therefore, decide which homes are suitable and schedule the meetings accordingly. Use the YMCA, parks, and camp for special events.

Invitations

By the third year, this practice may have worn a bit thin. However, the host team should still send out notices of the meeting. Use ingenuity and creativity to make the project of invitations fun for all.

Sports and Games

Some good parent-child games are possible, as long as you keep the emphasis on fun. Relays, bicycle contests, swim events, running and jumping contests, and the basics of team sports are possible activities.

Trips

Children this age may be getting interested in the why and how of things. Trips include more technical subjects, and the children gain real insights into how and why things work. Play to their interests. Visits to zoos or farms, nature centers, airports, docks, and science centers are fun and educational.

Ceremonies

Develop some of your own ideas. Spiritual expression can take on real meaning for the children. Poems, prayers, and music shared by children and parents can provide inspirational experiences.

Third Year

- Children participate in more advanced projects, as their capabilities have grown.
- Children lead games, stories, and songs.
- The group supports peer-group relationships.
- The group has more camping adventures and participates in group service.
- Parents appraise their children's development.

 # PARENT EDUCATION

Opportunities exist at every step of the Y-Indian Guide Programs for parents to learn new skills. For example, parents may learn more about dealing with children the same age as their own son or daughter; working in groups; developing leadership; becoming expert at crafts; organizing, scheduling, and planning; and handling social relationships.

Tribes can also build into this program a design for more formal education, enlisting the professional help of YMCA staff and community consultants. Fathers, mothers, and families will recognize the areas in which they need more guidance on any specific topic as they continue to meet. Each tribe is best able to diagnose and plan for itself the kinds of educational projects that will be most satisfying.

RECOGNITION AND AWARDS

Recognition is important to children and parents alike. One way tribal accomplishments can be recognized is through words and expressions of praise. A smile from Dad or Mom, a pat on the back, a word of approval from the Chief—all can have real meaning. Another way tribe members can be recognized is through the granting of awards. While awards can be fun for both the giver and receiver, they have some dangers.

Tribes may feel pressured to develop award systems. It may be hard to decide upon fair guidelines and to avoid overemphasizing awards at the expense of enjoying the experience. Awards may become routine; not all games, events, and projects need to conclude with awards. In addition, young children often do not understand the meaning of awards. Honest praise from a parent can be more satisfying to a child than the presentation of a blue feather.

Yet there are times when awards can be useful and necessary. The tribe may truly want to express esteem or appreciation in a concrete way. Honor in giving and honor in receiving is a part of American Indian culture.

Awards, if used in Y-Indian Guide Programs, should be available to all and should reflect personal growth and achievement, service to others, and full support of the tribe. They should not replace the real thrill and excitement of vibrant parent-child relationships and experiences. Honor in giving and receiving should be a crucial factor in any award or recognition ceremony. Parents will want to examine their feelings about recognition carefully before accepting an awards plan.

The following guidelines regarding gamesmanship and awards may be helpful to your tribe:

- In team play, help everyone feel like a winner.
- Do not strive for awards but for involvement.
- Set your mind on the game or project, not on gaining personal attention.
- Be concerned with the value and teachings of the game, not with the score.
- Accept an award with honor and present the next award with the same seriousness.

Indian Theme

The American Indian contributed greatly to our nation's Bill of Rights, introduced western Europeans to many new and important foods, originated new art and craft forms, and provided a living example of the courageous, self-sufficient individual in the wilderness. Yet most parents and children have little knowledge of the significant contributions by American Indians to our nation's history and heritage. The Y-Indian Guide Programs provide families with opportunities to learn about the American Indian culture and way of life. Parents and children will have a common base for interaction and learning, and tribes will gain a sense of unity and a foundation for productive activity.

Tribes should follow these steps as they participate in Y-Indian Guide Programs.

- Take time to learn about American Indians. Visit your local library for accurate information.
- Be sincere and look for the authentic in Indian culture—crafts, symbols, clothing.
- Recognize that Indians live today, not just in the past, and that each tribe is different.
- Solicit American Indian counsel to help you in your studies and tribal activities.
- Respect Indian-based ceremonies and religion.
- Support projects of human need and rights for Indian youth and families.
- Use your best judgment and taste in wearing Indian clothing and jewelry.

AMERICAN INDIAN CULTURAL VALUES AND PROGRAM DEVELOPMENT

The American Indian cultural theme gives the non-Indian parent a common interest and learning experience in working with a young child. As parents and children learn about and use Indian arts, crafts, games, songs, and stories, they gain a deeper appreciation for the achievements of another culture. Understanding people who have a different way of life builds strength, tolerance, openness, and wisdom among parents and children alike.

The genuine concern among Indian people for parent responsibility in teaching and guiding their sons and daughters to adulthood is a fine standard for non-Indian parents and children to live by in contemporary society. Teaching values, proper attitudes, fitness, knowledge, and ethics to the child is an integral part of the Indian way of life. Some of their strongest values include the following:

- A profound sense of responsibility for the well-being of all family members. They share their possessions with those who are in need.

- A high moral sense of human dignity and honor. Their given word is sacred, and honesty in all dealings is highly prized.
- Resourcefulness in using whatever nature has provided and gratitude for the blessings of nature.
- Physical endurance and personal self-control. Children are taught patience and self-control as part of their way of life.
- A high priority on things of the spirit. Their appreciation for the Creator is evident in their religion, traditions, and way of life.
- A deep understanding that all things in nature are interdependent. They realize we must conserve resources and eliminate waste so that future generations will enjoy the natural world the Creator has given us.
- Love of beauty, craftsmanship, and artistic skill. These qualities are honored in every tribe.
- Joy in games and sports. The primary stress is placed on involving all members of the tribe rather than on striving for awards.

The exact nature and content of each Y-Indian tribe's activity will vary considerably as its members seek to develop a program related to the needs and interests of all parents and children. However, there seems to be a certain magic for both parent and child as they share a campfire together; listen to the stories of the Iroquois; sleep in a hogan, chickee, or tepee; share in making Navajo jewelry; paddle a canoe; or play a Choctaw game.

The past and present culture of American Indians challenges parents in two ways: (a) to be aware of their roles as parent, guide, friend, and example for their children; and (b) to develop young boys' and girls' natural curiosity and enthusiasm for life.

THE AMERICAN INDIANS' CULTURAL HERITAGE

The name *Indian* was applied to native Americans by a Spanish explorer who mistakenly thought they were inhabitants of an Asian land. Today, an Indian is a person recognized as such by the Indian tribe with which he or she claims affiliation. A tribe is identified as a group of people, bound together by blood ties, who are socially, politically, and/or religiously organized and who usually speak a common language or dialect. On the basis of this definition, there are an estimated 6,716,000 American Indians living in the United States at this time, with slightly more than one-half of them on reservations and the rest in various cities throughout the country.

According to non-Indian scholars, the American Indian has lived on the North American continent for at least 10,000 years and probably for 35,000 years. At the time of Columbus's arrival in 1492, it is estimated that the Indian population was 834,000, although it had declined sharply to about 243,000 at the beginning of the twentieth century. Some 428 different tribes, bands, and groups have been recorded in the United States, representing a wide diversity of languages and customs.

There have been, and are today, many different American Indian tribes. Each tribe has lived according to its own distinct culture, language, habits, and customs. The food, shelter, arts, crafts, and clothing of each tribe depended on the materials available in their areas.

Six main groups of Indians, present at the time of the Europeans' arrival, have been identified on the basis of how they obtained their food:

- *Eastern Woodsmen:* from Maine to Florida, from the Atlantic to the Mississippi River, and from the Great Lakes and eastern Canada to the Gulf of Mexico.
- *Hunters of the Plains:* west of the Mississippi River to the Rocky Mountains.
- *Northern Fishermen:* along the Pacific Coast from northern California to southern Alaska.
- *Village Dwellers of the Southwest:* Arizona and New Mexico.
- *Nomads of the Southwest:* Arizona and New Mexico.
- *Seed Gatherers:* southern Rockies, Utah, southern California, and Nevada.

At the same time, seven American Indian cultural areas have been identified on the basis

Culture areas and approximate location of American Indian tribes. (Map originally published by the Indian Arts and Crafts Board.)

of language. (See map above.) These categories are similar to those based on food sources.

Today, the distinctions among the various American Indian tribes are even more pronounced. They do not form a single, unified minority group. There are important differences among tribes, pueblos, and bands. Variations in customs, language, tradition, attitudes, behavior, beliefs, and values are frequently marked between urban and reservation Indians; traditionalist, Christian, and Native American Church members; and full-blood and mixed-blood Indians.

THE AMERICAN INDIAN TODAY

The family group is the basic unit of American Indian society. Several family groups form a clan; several clans comprise a band. A tribe is usually composed of multiple bands. Tribes

are part of a nation, such as the Apache Nation.

A few groups still live much as their ancestors did, whereas others live like their non-Indian neighbors in the city or on a reservation. Most live with a mixture of traditional and modern ways of life.

Indian children are required to go to school. They attend public schools, mission or private schools, or federal government day and boarding schools.

Although many Indians are bilingual, some know only their tribal language. For some Indian children, it has been difficult to progress in schools where only English is used.

Most American Indians living on reservations engage in farming, fishing, stock-raising, timber production, or arts and crafts. Their average standard of living is very low, however, and unemployment in most areas is high. Contrary to popular belief, Indians do not receive automatic payments from the government.

Indians are United States citizens. They may vote and hold office like other Americans. They work, worship, and travel without restrictions. Many Indian leaders have gained success in government, education, law, art, and business and have made important contributions to this nation.

The American Indian population is increasing in spite of serious health problems, among them infectious respiratory diseases, pneumonia, tuberculosis, and trachoma. Poverty, alcoholism, and a high suicide rate among youth are also serious problems.

All Y-Indian Guide Program tribes will want to acquaint their members with the current plight of the American Indian. Fathers, mothers, sons, and daughters need to understand the serious problems that face Indian families living in the cities as well as on the reservations.

One of the greatest tragedies in American history has been the mistreatment of the Indian. Chicanery, disrespect, and paternalism have marked America's dealings with the Indians and have brought great dismay to many genuinely concerned citizens. Y-Indian Guide Program families can help bring new understanding and change to a persistent problem in our nation's history.

AMERICAN INDIAN ORGANI- ZATIONS

The Bureau of Indian Affairs in the U.S. Department of the Interior is responsible for the trusteeship over most Indian lands and for provision of public services to Indian people. However, many tribes and reservations west of the Mississippi River are under state jurisdiction. The Bureau of Indian Affairs, through its seven Tribal Operations Offices (see Appendix for listing), can be a helpful resource for information about American Indian tribes.

In order to advance the rights and culture of American Indians, the following important national organizations have emerged along with many other regional and local units. (Addresses for these organizations are available in the Appendix.)

• American Indian Historical Society

• American Indian Movement (AIM)
• National Congress of American Indians (NCAI)
• National Council on Indian Opportunity (NCIO)
• National Indian Youth Council (NIYC)
• National Tribal Chairman's Association (NTCA)

These organizations can be helpful resources to local YMCAs that are interested in the current struggle, concerns, and needs of American Indian youth and families.

PRECAUTIONS FOR THE USE OF AMERICAN INDIAN CULTURE

Because Y-Indian Guide Programs have drawn heavily on the culture and customs of American Indian tribes, YMCA lay and staff program leaders must try to represent the American Indians' contributions to our nation's life and history accurately and positively. The following guiding principles are presented for consideration and implementation by local YMCA boards and parent-child program leaders. They are designed to strengthen Y-Indian tribal programs, special events, and community interpretation. These principles are fundamental to understanding the American Indian people.*

• *An American Indian is a human being.* Scripts, films, program pageants, and youth activities that portray American Indians and their life-style, culture, and customs should be carefully evaluated for appropriateness. Do they fully express the Indians' humanity?

---

*This statement was adapted from an outline prepared by the Urban Indian Development Association of Los Angeles and presented at the 35th National Longhouse Convention in Pittsburgh on April 23, 1972. Charles C. Kujawa, National Consultant.

- *American Indian religion is sound.* Each tribe had its own beliefs, which evolved over many thousands of years. These religious beliefs served American Indians both in times of plenty and in times of need; they were sacred and meaningful to each tribe, and must be treated with respect and reverence.

- *American Indian morals are of long standing.* The morals of the true American Indians were very idealistic. Each tribe had its own standards, which were strictly observed. The moral decline among some Indian tribes began with the introduction of liquor and dishonorable trading practices by whites.

- *Indian customs have special meaning.* Various Indian tribes observed many colorful and meaningful customs, and each tribe adhered to its own culture and beliefs. Misrepresentation of these would constitute a grave injustice to the American Indian.

- *The languages of American Indians are graphic.* Each tribe spoke its own dialect and took great pride in oratory. The language used was both poetic and expressive. However, it is advisable to use the English language when portraying the American Indian. Today, few understand the Indian languages, and fewer still portray them correctly, thus making the Indian appear inarticulate. Words such as *how* and *ugh* were not part of the Indian vocabulary and should never be used.

- *Indian music and songs portray Indian life.* Music and song played a large part in the lives of American Indians. Through them, Indians expressed their religious beliefs, offered thanks to the Great Spirit, summoned the council, and served their personal and social needs. Music and songs were not taken lightly; thus, whenever used, they should be authentic and should accurately convey the intended meaning.

- *Indian dances are highly expressive.* Dance also provided Indians with recreation and self-expression, relating deeds and events of importance to the Indians. Many dances represent birds and animals from which they were adopted; they were always used with great care and ceremony. Many dances also served to keep the Indians in the good physical condition necessary for their survival.

- *Indian costumes were symbolic.* Costumes were very colorful, with many depicting the birds, animals, and flowers of the area in which the tribe lived. Costumes also had meaning in their design and color, serving as signs of rank and distinction for deeds of great valor. They should be depicted with authenticity.

- *The American Indian has a point of view.* Whenever written materials, scripts, telecasts, and visual aids concerning the American Indian are set forth, they should be made from the Indian point of view. Their values should be considered; their traditions respectfully upheld. Their interpretation of history should also be presented.

- *Indian leadership can create Indian roles.* Society has bypassed the American Indian. Non-Indians make and import Indian crafts, and produce and play the roles of Indians in motion pictures and TV programs about the American Indian. Non-Indians have also written and shaped Indian history and culture. There are many highly skilled and qualified American Indians who could have filled these roles. Unfortunately, the Indians have been alienated while their rich heritage has been exploited.

- *There is a real danger in stereotyping.* Hollywood's stereotype of the American Indian is a gross distortion. Ironically, this image is presented by the mass media to the public, who accept it as the truth. The motion picture industry and other groups, therefore, must take great care to present an accurate portrayal of American Indian heritage. Each Indian is an individual with individual mannerisms, guided by tribal beliefs and customs. YMCA Indian Guide groups should beware of perpetuating stereotypes of Indians in their newsletters, parades, and tribal activities.

- *Indian names should engender respect.* Names such as *squaw, buck* and *chief* are often used as nicknames: The Indian finds this degrading. Indians should be addressed with respect, by their proper names. Titles used in publicity and other materials should be respectful to Indians. Epithets such as "drunken Indian" must be avoided; they tend to label the whole Indian nation. In every case one must be discreet in the use of titles, considering how they relate to the well-being of, and respect for, the American Indian.
- *The Indian was not the aggressor in United States history.* Often American Indians are depicted as the aggressors in pictures, books, and films. It should be remembered that the white settlers and fur traders encroached upon the Indians, threatening their very existence and disregarding their hunting grounds and their rights as the original inhabitants of the land. Indians fought back against these intrusions. It was honorable to defend their homeland, as it is honorable to keep our nation free today. Therefore, it is not accurate to show the Indian always as the aggressor. In contrast, they should be shown as the defenders against white intruders who gave no consideration to the Indian way of life.
- *The American Indian was not a savage.* Many films, TV series, and books refer to the American Indian as a savage race. This abuse of the Indian culture is not accurate, and it should cease. The American Indians had established a very colorful and functional society. Unfortunately, the white race in most cases did not take time to learn and appreciate the Indian way of life.

YMCA lay and staff leaders are urged to use these guidelines in YMCA parent-child programs, policies, and practices; to establish small task groups for developing continuing educational and interpretive program opportunities for children and families; and to open up direct communication with nearby local Indian tribal councils for joint planning and sharing.

INDIAN SIGNS AND SYMBOLS

In the past, Indians used signs and symbols in ceremonies and as a means of sending messages, recording tribal history, and communicating with other tribes to overcome language barriers. Some of these symbols are included on the next few pages.

INDIAN DANCE STEPS

American Indian dancing has three characteristic foot movements or steps: the *toe-heel*, the *flat-heel*, and the *flat-foot*. These are regarded as basic movements. Each step has many variations and many related steps that are employed for the sake of variety.

The terms used to describe dance steps are those used in everyday conversation but with various shades of meaning. The following are brief definitions of these terms as they are used in this context.

- *Toe.* This means the ball of the foot, not the toe itself. For example, the instruction, "Place the toe down, with the heel raised," means to place the ball of the foot down with the heel raised off the floor.
- *Step.* A step as in walking; the stepping foot touches the ground before the other foot is raised. (In running, the advancing foot is still in the air when the other foot is raised.)
- *Hop.* This is done by standing on one foot, making a short spring, and landing on the same foot.
- *Trot.* A short spring from one foot to the other in a relaxed run, in which the advancing foot is still in the air when the other foot is raised.
- *Jump.* (1) A short spring from one foot to the other; (2) a spring on both feet at the same time.
- *Skip.* A low, short spring on one foot in which the foot is barely raised off the ground—a sort of push or scrape in which the ball of the foot brushes the ground.

	Snow Moon Jan.		Eagle		Camp
	Hunger Moon Feb.		Wolf		Town
	Crow Moon Mar.		Owl		Village
	Wild Goose Moon - April		Fish		Man
	Planting Moon May		Sign of Buffalo		Woman
	Rose Moon June		Council Fire		Child
	Thunder Moon July		Yesterday		Water
	Green Corn Moon Aug.		Tomorrow		Rain
	Hunting Moon Sept.		Good		Snow
	Falling Leaf Moon - Oct.		Live Bear		Sunrise
	Mad Moon Nov.		Dead Bear		Sunset
	Long Night Moon Dec.		Thunderbird		Sun or Day

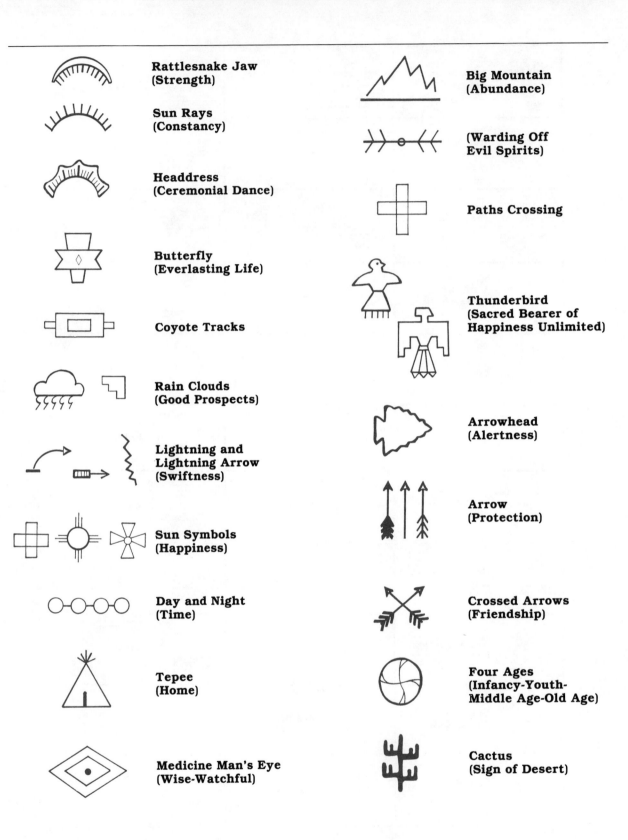

Rattlesnake Jaw (Strength)	Big Mountain (Abundance)
Sun Rays (Constancy)	(Warding Off Evil Spirits)
Headdress (Ceremonial Dance)	Paths Crossing
Butterfly (Everlasting Life)	Thunderbird (Sacred Bearer of Happiness Unlimited)
Coyote Tracks	
Rain Clouds (Good Prospects)	Arrowhead (Alertness)
Lightning and Lightning Arrow (Swiftness)	Arrow (Protection)
Sun Symbols (Happiness)	Crossed Arrows (Friendship)
Day and Night (Time)	Four Ages (Infancy-Youth-Middle Age-Old Age)
Tepee (Home)	Cactus (Sign of Desert)
Medicine Man's Eye (Wise-Watchful)	

Pictographs on this and the next two pages taken from *Key to Indian Pictographs*, Akwesasne Counselor Organization, St. Regis Mohawk Reservation, Hogansburg, New York.

Gila Monster
(Sign of Desert)

Cactus Flower
(Courtship)

Horse
(Journey)

Shaking Hands
(Friendship)

Saddle Bags
(Journey)

Bird
(Carefree,
Light-Hearted)

Lightning Snake
and Snake
(Defiance, Wisdom)

Thunderbird Track
(Bright Prospects)

Deer Track
(Plenty Game)

Bear Track
(Good Omen)

Crossed Arms
(Sleep)

"O'Chief"
(Sign of Recognition
in Council)

See, to See

Speaking

Spirit

Stars

Time, Sunrise

Time, Noon

Time, Sunset

Tree (More Than One
Indicates Forest)

Weather, Clear

Welcome, Sociability

Night

Woman

White Woman

Trail

Top Man With Eagle Feather in His Hand Denoting Power

Dust

Because

Therefore

Windy (Moon in Circle)

Male

Female

Young

Quiet

Weather, Bad

Thunder and Lightning

Lamp of Beauty

Lamp of Fortitude

Lamp of Truth

Lamp of Service

War

- *Tap.* (1) A pat on the ground with the ball of the foot, the foot being immediately raised again; (2) a pat on the ground with the heel, the heel being immediately raised again.
- *Beat.* One beat of the drum.
- *Count.* A unit of drumming that would be expressed as one count. In unaccented drumming it is one beat of the drum. In two-time drumming, accented *loud-soft*, it is the unit of loud and soft beats, counted "one-and" and so forth.
- *Powwow dancing.* Dancing in which each dancer is free to dance as he or she chooses, using whatever appropriate movements are desired without following a fixed routine.

- *Group dance.* A dance with a fixed routine in which each dancer performs essentially the same movements at the same time.
- *Story dance.* A dance depicting a story.
- *"I Saw" dance.* A story dance reenacting an exploit or happening, presumably one that the dancer saw or experienced.

Fundamental Steps

The three basic steps are described here, first in their simple form and then with the two-foot action.

The Toe-Heel Step

& (soft beat)   Place left toe down, heel raised.

1 (loud beat)   Drop left heel, simultaneously raising right foot.

& (soft beat)   Place right toe down, heel raised.

2 (loud beat)   Drop right heel, simultaneously raising left foot.

This universal movement is characteristic of the dancing of the tribes of the northern Woodlands and northern Plains. It is the best foundation for the other dancing styles and thus we recommend that you start with this step when you learn dances as a tribe.

To achieve the proper movement, you must keep your feet under your body at all times. The following figure illustrates both the right (A) and the wrong (B) positions of the feet.

When the foot is extended far forward as in B, the heel cannot be brought down gracefully and naturally, and the step will seem awkward and strained.

With the feet at the proper position, lower the body a little by bending the knees to the angle shown in A. The knees remain bent at approximately this angle at all times during the step. They are never straightened out.

With the weight on the right foot, place the ball of the left foot down about six inches forward, keeping the heel elevated at the natural height. Drop the left heel down and simultaneously lift the right foot for the next step. As the left heel is brought down, *the left knee bends or gives a little.* To use the dancing term, the knee is *soft.* The heel is not forced down by using the leg muscles but by dropping the weight of the body on it. In placing the left toe forward, the weight is on the right foot; then it is suddenly transferred to the left, thus dropping the heel down hard, the knee flexing to take up the jar. To the extent that the legs are kept relaxed and the knee soft, the step becomes easy, natural, and fluid. Thus it is more of an up-and-down movement than a forward or gliding one. Relaxed as it should be, the whole body shakes up and down a little on each step.

The step is done to two-time drumming, accented loud-soft. *Place the toe down on the soft beat and drop the heel on the loud beat.* The accent of the loud beat is an aid to bringing the heel down emphatically.

The Flat-Heel Step

& (soft beat)   Step forward with left foot flat on floor.

1 (loud beat)   Raise left heel and drop it down on count.

& (soft beat)   Step forward with right foot flat on floor.

2 (loud beat)   Raise right heel and drop it down on count.

The feet hug the ground. They are raised no higher than necessary in stepping and are brought down flat; the heel is raised very little before the heel tap. The weight stays on the heels all the time. Steps should be short so as not to straighten out the legs. If toes are turned up so that they touch the top of the shoe or moccasin, it is easier to put the foot down absolutely flat.

Essential points to keep in mind: Keep your feet flat, hugging the ground; knees bent to keep feet under the body; soft knee, flexing when weight is placed on it; heel raised by an upward lift of the body; and heel lowered by dropping weight on it.

The Flat-Foot Step

1 (loud beat)	Step on left foot flat.
& (soft beat)	Skip on left foot flat.
2 (loud beat)	Step on right foot flat.
& (soft beat)	Skip on right foot flat.

The feet are flat at all times; they are brought down flat on both the step and the skip, and the sole of the foot is flat or parallel to the floor when raised. The knees are kept slightly bent.

Keeping the feet flat, step forward on the left, raising the right; skip forward on the left as the right advances, then repeat with the right. On the *skip*, the foot is barely raised off the floor, brushing the floor as it goes forward; but on the *step*, the foot is raised to a height of about six inches. The body is erect and sways from side to side naturally with the step. There is no heel action, no pounding of the floor, and no hugging the floor with the feet.

Handling the Arms

The most common position of the arms is hanging naturally at the sides, fully relaxed, as shown by the first position in the following figure. The second most common position is *in front of the chest*, shown in positions A, B, and C. The hands are held in front of the chest, separated by a few inches, and move in reflex fashion with the fingers loosely joined or with both hands holding some small object. Elbows hang close to the sides, with the arms and hands completely relaxed.

It's a great help in dancing to have small objects in the hands, such as eagle wing fans, feathers, dance rattles, or peace pipes.

The Full Crouch

The full crouch is the climax or extreme of close-to-the-ground dancing. It is used not as a fundamental movement, but as a brief moment of spectacle or splash of color. The full crouch is most effective when the dancer suddenly drops into it from the upright position.

You do not move forward, backward, or to the side when in the crouch. It is dancing on the spot, involving nothing more in the way of footwork than raising the heels and jarring them down. Go into the full crouch, bending the trunk forward parallel to the ground; spread the legs well apart, the knees sticking outward a little, as shown in the following figure. Drop the arms between the legs, with the hands close to the ground and fists closed. Keep the back flat and the shoulders straight.

In this position, shake hard up and down to the drumming, raising heels and jarring them down. Heels are raised not by feet alone, but by an up-and-down motion of the entire body.

It is effective to hold rattles in your hands and shake them down as though striking at the ground with each drumbeat but never quite touching the ground.

Dances

The following two dances are good for beginners. To avoid embarrassing the children, parents should join in learning the dances. This also makes the dancing more enjoyable for them.

Oto Rabbit Dance

Always an interesting and entertaining dance, the Rabbit Dance of the Otos is an active, fast-paced activity that both parents and children can enjoy. Eight to twelve dancers can participate. They enter the ring and stroll along in disinterested fashion awaiting the drumming. When the drumming starts, they drop instantly to the right knee and shake the body up and down for sixteen counts. Then they rise and dance strenuously for thirty-two counts.

The drumming is counted "*one*-and-*two*-and," with each unit (one-and or two-and) regarded as one count.

1. Sixteen counts—drumming fast, soft, unaccented. Each dancer drops to the right knee and shakes up and down with much shoulder motion, once to each beat.

2. Thirty-two counts—drumming changes to loud, accented two-time. The dancers leap to their feet and dance strenuously, using the toe-heel step and employing vigorous, expressive body action. Each dancer stays near his or her original spot.
3. Sixteen counts—repeat Step 1
4. Thirty-two counts—repeat Step 2
5. Sixteen counts—repeat Step 1
6. Exit by rising and trotting out.

The drumming is fast, and the tempo remains constant throughout, although it may change in accent and volume from one step to the next. For the shaking step, the drumming is soft, rapid, and unaccented. For the dancing step, it becomes loud and accented in two-time. This indicates the change from one step to the next, and the dancers react immediately to the change.

The Chippewa Serpentine Dance

This is an ideal dance for beginners, for it resembles the familiar "Follow the Leader" game.

A good dancer should be the leader. He or she should start with the toe-heel step and change to various steps as the dance progresses. Any number of dancers may take part.

As in the old Grand March, the dancers first move around in a large circle, then across the stage, forming large figure eights as they weave in and out. To make the dance effective, the dancers should be evenly spaced, changing steps only at a loud drum signal. The trick of this fun dance is to change steps immediately at the change in the drum beat. The tempo varies from slow to fast.

The dance is spectacular when danced in perfect unison, ending with the dancers' turning in the last steps to face the audience.

Invitations

Every parent-child team gets several turns in the course of a year to make and deliver invitations. This task is often considered a bother rather than a good opportunity to achieve Y-Indian Guide purposes. The following suggestions can help make creating invitations a time for parents and children to work together and to learn more about tribal and Native Indian lore.

- Choose a theme for the invitation that relates to Indians or nature. It need not be elaborate or realistic.
- Design an invitation that both you and your child can work on together. For example, a paper tepee that the little Brave/Princess/Maiden has decorated is much better than a real leather one that Mom or Dad created alone.
- Keep the project simple so that the task of making invitations for the whole tribe is not too lengthy or difficult.

- Allow enough time, probably two evenings, so that the project will be fun and the little Brave/Princess/Maiden will have invitations of which he or she can be proud.
- Try out invitations that will encourage the other parents and children to work together also, such as putting one bell on a rawhide thong along with a tag telling the meeting time and place. By adding more bells and some fur or leather, parents and children can make this invitation into ankle bells for an Indian costume.
- Use authentic Indian sign language and symbols as much as possible (see illustration below).
- If you have exhausted the ideas presented in this manual, additional resources are available at your YMCA or local library.
- Deliver the invitation to each home together with your son or daughter. Talk with your child about what it means to be a host, and the fun you had in making the invitations.

| COUNCIL | (at) | TEPEE | (of) | BIG FOX | and | LITTLE FOX | 12th |

| SUN (DAY) | THUNDER MOON (July) | 7:30 | (at) | NIGHT. |

IDEAS FOR MEETING INVITATIONS

Scissors, paper, and crayons can give you an endless variety of invitation designs and do not require much of your time. Here are some good ideas that other tribes have used:

Paint brush

Stretched hide

Sun, moon, or stars

Animal tracks

Animal that represents Indian name of host

Stick-on stars in familiar constellations

Shirts

Campfires

Trees

Moccasins

Tools (for handicraft meetings)

Indian silhouettes

Tepees

Tomahawks

Arrows

Quivers

Headdresses

Leaves

Feathers

Seasonal symbols

Animal silhouettes

Pottery

Drums

Navajo designs

Shields

Snowshoes

Peace pipe

Corn

Totem poles

Arrowheads

Wooden paddle

Bookmarker

Birch bark card

If you want to get fancy, you can incorporate some of the following ideas into your own projects: straw bundles, miniatures such as a bow-and-arrow set, moccasins stitched with embroidery thread, wooden knives, and tomahawk or drum cutouts. An inverted, cone-shaped paper cup with a bit of red-dyed cotton batting for a fire makes a realistic tepee. Also, objects from nature such as feathers, leaves, unusual rocks, shells, bones, and pinecones make excellent invitations.

A very successful meeting has been built around a plaster mold invitation that was brought to the meeting and painted. Another good idea was a lollipop with a paper face, feather, and hair attached with tape.

INVITATIONS TO MAKE

The following ideas for invitations have provided parents and children with hours of creative fun and learning opportunities. Try your hand at any one of these designs. They are constructed from materials you may have around the house or can obtain easily such as aluminum foil, balsawood, boxes, cans, cardboard, cork, leather, paper, pipe cleaners, plastic, rubber, and paper.

Potato Print Invitation

Cut a small potato in half. Have your little Brave/Princess/Maiden draw an Indian design or message on a piece of paper and cut it out to fit the potato. Lay it in the center of the cutside of the potato. Incise the edges of the design about ½'' deep with a small knife. Remove the background a bit at a time until the design stands out. Color the design using a stamp pad or painting food coloring on the design with a brush. Press the design down on the paper you have selected for printing the invitations; then lift the design straight up.

Remember, designs will print in reverse, so make sure you spell any words on the design backwards so that they read in the right direction. You and your child could each make an Indian design and print them in two colors on paper that has been cut into the shape of an animal pelt or tepee. This is lots of fun and simple!

Cork Alligator

String various-sized corks from head to tail with wire or hairpins. Slit the tail cork to insert a stiff paper tail. Use tacks for eyes and legs. Make a slit in the head cork for the mouth. Put the invitation in the mouth.

Scroll

Split two sticks, each about ¾" in diameter and 6" long, lengthwise. After inserting the ends of your scroll paper between the two split sides, tack or glue the sticks back together to hold the paper firmly. Write your invitation on the scroll. Decorate the four ends of sticks with colored twine, feathers, and the like.

Indian Spurs

Cut two strips from flexible cardboard 1" wide and 13" long. Make a notch at each end of the strips for fastening around the ankle. Have your child make designs and write the invitation on the spurs. You can also paste aluminum foil on the rowel of the spur to make it look more realistic.

The Indian Turtle That Swims

This is an invitation that will have them talking! Draw and cut out a paper turtle from notebook paper. Make a small round hole in the center of the turtle and cut a narrow slit leading from the center hole to the tail. Dip the lower half of the turtle into water. Lay the turtle gently on the surface of the water in a bowl or tub. To make it swim, drop a little oil

(1 or 2 drops) into the hole. The oil will start to spread through the slit and the turtle will move forward. In the invitation, your little Brave/Princess/Maiden can promise to make the Indian turtle swim following refreshments.

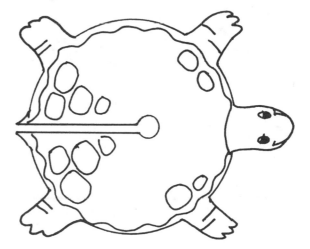

Eskimo Igloo

This can also be a fun short tribal project. Take half of an eggshell or a "L'eggs" (stockings) eggshell package and draw lines on it with a pencil to represent blocks of snow. Paint a little entrance at the bottom. Dip the bottom edge of the shell in glue and place it on a piece of cotton, or have the whole tribe whip up a village on a larger piece of cotton. You can follow with a story about the Eskimos.

Indian Skinning Knife

Get tongue depressors from the drugstore and trace the outline of a skinning knife on the wood. Cut or sand excess wood away and sand an edge on the blade. The handle can be decorated by woodburning, wrapping it in colored string, or painting on designs.

Arrows

Use a small stick or dowel for the shaft of the arrow and cut a slot in one end. Cut out an arrowhead from drawing paper, print the invitation on it, and insert the paper in the shaft slot. Make arrow feathers out of paper, yarn, or bird feathers.

Arrowheads

Cardboard, aluminum sheeting, wood, paper, Styrofoam, or even a rock may be used as the base material for arrowheads. The invitation can be decorated with colorful paints or stamped with a metal punch.

Canoe

For this design you'll need a piece of 4" x 6" heavy paper. Fold the paper in half lengthwise and draw the canoe design on the paper with the bottom of the canoe along the fold. Cut the canoe out and glue the ends together. Have two wooden matchsticks on hand to use as seats. Print the invitation on the outside of the canoe, then glue the two matchsticks near the bow and stern.

Alternative: Use a 6" piece of balsawood to make a dugout canoe. Instruct your child in the proper use of a carving knife before you begin cutting. You can use a woodburning tool both to decorate and to print the invitation.

Drum

A small can (those used for tomato paste, baby food, etc. are ideal) is the drum base with rubber or leather stretched across the top and bottom. The rubber or leather may be tied or glued on, with the invitation printed on the top or sides.

Feather

This is a good beginning project for children and their parents. You can use paper for drawing or cutting out a feather. Inscribe the invitation with crayons or marking pens. You can also use felt flannel for the feather, with symbols cut out of different colors of felt and glued to the feather.

Headband

Designing a special invitation headband of leather, cloth, or paper can be fun for parent and child alike. The invitation written in Indian symbols provides a warm welcome to neighborhood friends.

Hide or Skin

Cut an 8" x 11" piece of leather, vinyl, or cloth in the shape of an animal hide. Paint symbols for the message in the center. Roll it up and put it in a tube or a wooden napkin ring for carrying. Alternative: Stretch the hide out flat between 4 twigs and tie them with thread or twine.

Log Chip
Saw a 4''-diameter fireplace log into pieces about ½'' thick. Inscribe the invitation on the face of the chip with a woodburning tool or paint.

Indian Travois
Obtain a small plastic horse. With small strips of adhesive tape, fasten 2 sticks to the horse (lollipop sticks work well), 1 on each side. Apply the tape so that it looks like a harness. Cut a piece of paper for the travois, write the invitation on it, and tape or glue the paper to both sticks.

Map
Design an 8'' x 11'' map that gives directions to the host's home. You can use drawing paper, cardboard, cloth, or plywood. Create a legend to identify the symbols you use, if necessary. Let your imagination run free with this design.

Moccasin
A paper drawing or a 4'' leather cutout of a moccasin works well. Decorate the cutout with beads or bells and paint or draw the message on the moccasin.

Necklace
Acorns, beads, or shells that have been collected on a trip to the woods, beach, or store can be strung together on waxed string or twine. Tie a message tag on one end.

Paddle
Cut the shape of a canoe paddle out of a thin wooden stick or shingle; then sand rough edges. Write the date, time, place of meeting, and hosts' names on the paddle blade. You can also use felt, cardboard, or tin in place of the wood.

Pinecones
Take a hike in the woods to collect pinecones or draw your own. Attach ribbon and bells to each pinecone along with a message tag. This design is a good holiday project. You can paint your real pinecones and add glitter to make them look more festive.

Quiver
Make a tube container from a juice can or paper roll. Decorate the outside with magazine picture cutouts or painted designs, felt, flannel, or aluminum foil. Attach a string carrier. Make an arrow from a small stick (see "Arrow" instructions above) and attach the invitation to the arrow.

Snowman
A Styrofoam ball about 2'' in diameter serves as the snowman's head. Its hat can be designed from paper or felt. Facial features of shiny colored paper can be pasted into place. The message is printed on small notepaper, folded over, and tucked into the top of the snowman's hat.

Tepee
Design a small tepee from a cone-shaped cup, bright construction paper, or aluminum foil. Insert three twigs or sticks for poles. Decorate with Indian symbols. Glue the tepee to a 4'' x 6'' cardboard base. Write your invitation on the base.

Tree Leaves
Use scrap pieces of colored leatherette, heavy construction paper, or bristol board for cutting out elm, maple, oak, basswood, ginko, poplar, or ash leaves to actual size. Trace in veins of the leaf. Inscribe the invitation on the leaf's blank side. In some cases, you can use actual leaves.

Animal or Bird Pictures
Use drawing paper, leather, or cardboard and paint or crayons. Draw a picture of a bear, deer, mountain lion, blue jay, or other animal

or bird and cut out the design. Print your invitation on the cutout and decorate with Indian symbols or colored designs.

Animal Tracks
Draw beaver, bear, deer, dog, raccoon, or other animal tracks on cardboard, heavy construction paper, or plywood. Print the invitation across the track in bright colors.

Bookmarker
This is a good beginning project. Cut the bookmarker out of cloth, leather, or plastic. Depict the message on the bookmarker with Indian symbols.

Tribal Property

Every tribe should make its own tribal property, purchasing the material with the tribal wampum. Property is usually kept in the tribal property box. Following each meeting, the next host takes the property box to his or her home so that tribal property is always on hand at the site of each successive meeting.

Each parent and child should share some of the responsibility for making part of the tribal property. For example, the Tallykeeper makes the tallykeeper's book, the Wampum Bearer makes the wampum pouch, and so on. Two families might work together on the larger items. You can decide how the property is to be made in the parents' meetings. The important point is to get your property made as quickly as possible, with everyone sharing some of the responsibility.

BASIC TRIBAL PROPERTY

The basic tribal property for each tribe may include the following:

Totem pole

Ceremonial Indian shield

Wampum (money) pouch

Talking stick or rock

Tribal drum

Council fire

Tribal property box

Tallykeeper's book

Coup stick

Tribal standard

Totem Pole
Although original totems were carved out of huge tree trunks, in the Y-Indian Guide Programs, simpler methods are used. First, we suggest that you do some research to find out exactly what design or styles were used by the Indians from whom your tribal name was adopted.

The totem pole is one of the most important tribal properties. Each family decorates its own section. This section is taken to and from the council meeting by each family and placed on the totem at the beginning of the meeting. By placing your block on the totem, you indicate your presence at the council.

Totem poles can be made quite easily from one-gallon cans. These cans, when decorated, stand supported by a central dowel, and make a good first totem. As your tribe becomes more interested in crafts and wants to make a more ambitious totem pole, you might consider the following project.

One parent should take responsibility for going to the lumberyard and purchasing a piece of 6'' x 6'' lumber long enough so that each

TOP VIEW

ASSEMBLY

SECTIONS MAY BE DOWELED OR MOUNTED ON A CENTER PIPE

BASE

BASE

3 DIMENSIONAL EFFECTS CAN BE ACHIEVED WITH VERY LITTLE CARVING

WINGS

family in your tribe will have a section. We recommend a soft wood, like pine or redwood, that is easy to work with. If the parent does not have an electric saw, he or she should have someone at the lumberyard cut the wood into uniform lengths. The next step is to drill a hole ½" deep and ¾" to 1" in diameter in each end of each length. A 3"-long dowel is then glued in the bottom hole so that the pieces can be stacked one on top of the other, with the dowels holding them in place.

Each family then receives its section. The son or daughter in the family should sand down the four sides for finishing. The totem is now ready for decorating. Many tribes put the tribal name on one side of the totem, one letter to each block, if possible. Use your imagination in decorating the other sides with a woodburning tool or paints.

Make a base as a stand for the totem. The tribe may decide later to make a top piece, such as a spread eagle. We suggest that families not try difficult carvings. It is best to keep the totem pole simple and complete it as quickly as possible. Each family should bring its totem pole section to each meeting, even if they are still in the process of decorating it, so that members can share ideas and see how each family is progressing.

It is not essential that each tribe use the same materials or follow the patterns described above. In some cases, tribes have used nail kegs, lard cans, large (No. 10) vegetable cans, and many other items for totem poles. Originality is important in constructing tribal property.

Ceremonial Indian Shield

The following materials are needed for this project: stiff white cardboard (enough for a 16"-diameter circle); plywood circle of the same size; colored sand; four 6" feathers; fluff feathers; a large stick; dyed horse hair or colored yarn (optional); a drill or punching tool; a large stapler or hammer and nail; string; and glue.

Cut out a cardboard circle and glue it to a plywood circle for strength. Draw symbols representing tribal designs, individual names, or the seasons. Some tribes have each child draw out a representation of one of the six aims and explain in meetings what it means to him or her.

Cover the designs with bright sand painting (see instructions for sand painting in the "Crafts" section). Finish the shield by decorating it with feathers. Holes are punched to tie the feathers at the four corners, with 3" intervals between them. Four 6" feathers represent the four directions, the colors of which are North—yellow; East—red; South—blue; West —white. Smaller fluff feathers are hung from the holes between the four corners. Glue a tuft of dyed horse hair or colored yarn to the center of the shield if desired. Fasten a handle to the center of the back with a staple or nail.

You can also make these shields from canvas and paint them with oil paints. They are very colorful and add dignity and color to public affairs, particularly inductions, where they are mounted on tripods to be displayed. The National Longhouse has suggested that tribes may make these shields instead of totem poles.

Wampum (Money) Pouch

This is a container for holding the tribe's funds. Usually a drawstring is inserted to close the pouch. Decorate the pouch with beads and paint, using original designs created by both parent and child. The pouch can be either fastened on the belt or carried in the hand.

You can use chamois, imitation leather, or heavy felt to make the pouch. Sew the edges together with heavy thread. Insert cord or leather thong for the drawstring. Fringe the bottom, then decorate as desired. Other pouch designs are possible. Several types are suggested below.

Talking Stick or Rock

No two talking sticks or rocks are alike. This project can tap the creative imagination of the tribe. Using a stick or a strong, round rock found on a tribal hike, parents and children proceed to paint and decorate it with feathers, beads, leather, or other decorating materials.

The purpose of the talking stick or rock is to grant a tribal member permission to speak at a meeting. The person who is speaking holds it in his or her hands. Everyone else must listen until that person finishes. The talking stick or rock is then passed on to the next speaker. The stick or rock can also be placed in front of the member who is to speak.

Tribal Drum

The tribal drum is an indispensable piece of equipment for the tribe. Tribal participation in making the drum builds a strong feeling of ownership and teamwork. The drum is used regularly in meeting ceremonies, and it should not be considered a toy. The tribe should make and use it with care, for it is one of the principal Native American musical instruments.

There are several ways to make a tribal drum. You can make a good body for the drum

Stick in slot

Flap

Paint tribal designs on front side -- or use some beadwork -- or make with fur -- or woodburn

Make from two pieces of leather -- the back a few inches longer to form flap

Leather Thong

Sew two identical halves together and turn inside out -- then fringe

Beadwork

Sew Here

Fringe the bottom

Cut circle of leather -- attach drawstring -- paint

from a clean, tight wooden nail keg, a round cheesebox, or a large tin can. Be sure to make the drum small enough to fit into the tribal property box (described later). Rawhide makes a good drum head. The rawhide should be about 2" or 3" larger than the diameter of the body. You can use any scraps left over from the head for thongs.

The body of the drum should be smooth; pad the ends where the head will be stretched with a thin layer of cloth or soft leather. Seal any holes or leaks through which air may escape as tightly as possible in order to preserve the good tone of the drum.

Soak the rawhide in warm water for about 4 to 6 hours. Frequently changing the water helps remove dirt and other matter left on the hide. Cut two circles out of the rawhide that are a few inches larger in diameter than the diameter of the body. Then cut a series of holes around each circle of rawhide 1" from the edge and 3" apart. These holes should be in the shape of a narrow "V" with the point facing the circumference of the circle.

Place the body with one end sitting on one of the heads and the other end covered by the other head. With thongs cut from scraps of wet rawhide, begin lacing diagonally through the holes cut in the heads. When the lacing reaches around to where you began, have someone hold the two thong ends together while you go back around and take up all the slack in the thong. Tie the loose ends together with a secure square knot. Let the drum dry slowly and evenly. Coat the uncured rawhide with a protective layer of clear varnish to retard deterioration. Decorate the drum with Indian symbols or other designs.

Make a beater for the drum at the same time. First wrap cotton cord or gauze bandage around a supple stick about 12" long. When finished, wrap the cotton or gauze with strips of adhesive tape; then cover with a piece of soft leather. Decorate the stick with feathers or beads.

Council Fire

Secure some small sticks, 10" to 14" long and 1" to 2" in diameter. They may be live or dry, depending on what you can find. (Do not cut down a live tree or bush for this purpose.) Take six to ten sticks and stack them in the form of a tepee, a log cabin fire, or a combination of both. Screw, nail, or tie the sticks together.

Mount a light socket in the center of a ½" to ¾" plywood base, and make sure the cord runs underneath the wood. Attach the sticks over the light socket. Use a small 25-watt red bulb to simulate a fire. The electric cord should be at least 12' to 14' long so that it will reach the center of any tribal council room. You can hold council around a campfire indoors with this device.

Tribal Property Box

This box should be large enough to hold all tribal property, yet small enough to handle easily. It should be a hinged, covered box with a latch so that it can be decorated. This box holds most of the tribal property, including totem pole, drum, campfire, and headbands. We recommend that you use plywood to construct this box. Even an old footlocker, painted and decorated, will make a very satisfactory chest. You may want to purchase a lock for the box as well.

Tallykeeper's Book

Keep records of councils and meetings in this book. It can be constructed easily by the Tallykeeper and his or her child. Secure 2 pieces of ½" plywood about 9" x 12" for the covers of the book. Drill 2 or 3 small ¼" holes along one side of both covers to accommodate loose-leaf sheets. Bind the covers together with leather thongs. Decorate the covers with a woodburning tool or paints and inscribe the tribal name on the front.

This book can also be used as the tribal scrapbook. Collect pictures of trips, outings, family events, and special activities to keep as a history of the tribe. It will grow in value as the months and years go by.

Coup Stick

Indians used the coup stick to welcome guests and show them hospitality. It is displayed *outside* the home. To make the coup stick, secure a 3' to 4' dowel or stick. The coup stick should be pointed at one end. Decorate the stick with a totem head, feathers (6" long), colored yarn, fur, painted designs, and the like.

Indians also used these sticks to indicate ownership. When moving from one hunting ground to another, they would drive the stick into the ground to mark their hunting areas as well as places where they had left their possessions. Other Indians, seeing the coup stick, knew at once by the decorations the name and tribal affiliation of the owner.

Tribal Standard

Tribes use the tribal standard to identify themselves at Longhouse events, special ceremonies, and camp-outs. Each parent and child can help make and decorate the staff and shield or banner. Select a pole or sapling about 4' long for the standard and banner. Attach a plywood shield or cloth banner; then paint tribal emblems and history on the standard. A colorful, attractive standard is a symbol of the tribe's unity.

 COSTUMES

Although costumes are not mandatory, they establish a sense of unity in the tribe and help participants get into the spirit of the program. Each tribe may decide on a costume, material, and style, and each parent and child can then make their own. The costume itself is not as important as the sharing and enjoyment that parents and children experience in making it.

The costumes include dresses, tunics or war shirts, decorations, headgear, shields, and jewelry. The clothing may be full dress with beads, fringe, and feathers or a simple cape or vest cut out of a gunnysack. You can also use a cotton-polyester blend or muslin (unbleached) as costume material. Try to choose a fabric that is easy to sew and that requires little or no ironing.

Tribal Tunic

Cut out a tunic (see illustration on next page) from an old pillowcase or piece of cloth. Lace the sides together with colored yarn or leather thongs. Use colorfast markers, colored yarn, and beads to decorate the tunic with Indian designs.

Indian Vest

To make the vest, you will need 1 yard of material for each parent and child—use either flannel, denim, canvas, rayon suede, leather, or wool. Secure 3 yards of ½" red flannel or bias tape for seam binding. Obtain yarn or embroidery cotton for designs and fringe (optional).

Trace a vest pattern on wrapping paper to fit each parent and child, one piece for the back and two for the front of the vest. Sew the

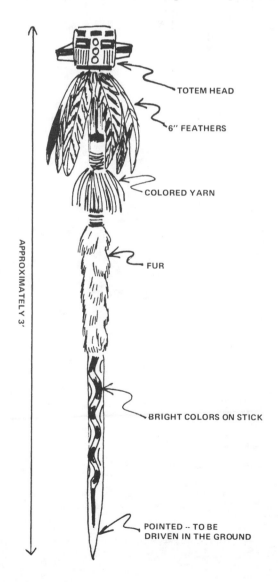

APPROXIMATELY 3'

TOTEM HEAD

6" FEATHERS

COLORED YARN

FUR

BRIGHT COLORS ON STICK

POINTED -- TO BE DRIVEN IN THE GROUND

CAMP PATCHES

TIE HERE

NECK OPENING AND FLAP WHICH GOES OVER IT

pattern together and fit it to the wearer, making adjustments where needed.

Trace the pattern onto the material and cut it out. Sew the pieces together and add the red flannel or bias tape as a seam binder. Decorate the vests and add fringe as desired. Each parent-child team can have its own design and pattern, or a tribe may develop similar vests to build unity in the group.

Trophy Shirt

Secure ½ yard of brown denim or flannel, flannel scraps for designs, 12 grommets, and 24'' of leather thong for fringe (optional).

Trace a pattern on wrapping paper and cut out to size, including a center head space. Pin the pattern on the material and cut out. Insert 12 grommets along the lower sides for lacing. Sew on Y-Indian Guide emblem, name patch, or other designs. Add fringe on the bottom if desired.

Leggings

You will need 2 yards of material, 24'' wide, in denim, rayon suede cloth, buckskin, or other heavy material. Secure 1½ yards of plastic beading, trim strip, or ribbon, and rayon felt or flannel for fringe.

Cut the legging pattern from wrapping paper and try on for the proper fit. Trace the pattern onto the material and cut it out. Pin the sides lengthwise and fit for sewing. Sew in the beaded strip before the legging seam is finished. Attach the fringe and sew up the legging seam. Finish by sewing on a loop at the top of the leggings to attach them to the wearer's belt.

Copper Rings

Take a 36'' length of No. 14 copper wire and double it. While you hold the loose ends with a pair of pliers, your child puts a nail through the copper loop at the other end. Pulling hard, your child turns the nail and twists the wire, winding it around itself like a braid. When it is fully twisted, it can be flattened with a hammer against a hard surface like an anvil. Twist the flattened copper into a ring and cut off to proper length. It can be wound once, twice, or three times around the finger. Polish the copper with steel wool either before or after twisting. Makes two rings.

Leather Thongs

You can obtain scrap leather from several sources: shoe-repair shops, shoe-making companies, leather works, and other companies that can be found in the phone book. The leather often comes in attractive colors.

To cut thongs you will need a cutting tool and gauge to make sure you cut the leather thong the same thickness from beginning to end. One you can make yourself requires a razor blade, a shingle, and a shingle nail. Set the razor blade in the butt end of the shingle and drive the shingle nail on one side of the razor as a spacer. Take the leather in both hands, hold it over the razor, and pull it toward you, with the outer edge touching the nail. If you have a small piece of leather you can still cut a fairly long leather thong by starting from the outer edge and cutting in one continuous spiral toward the center of the piece.

To straighten the thong, wet it thoroughly and tie each end so the length is loosely stretched between two poles, chairs, or other stationary objects. Put a light weight in the middle to take out the bends, and when the leather dries it will be straight.

Breechcloth

Breechcloths are the traditional apparel of the Indian dancer. They are made from a rectangular piece of flannel or other substantial material and are usually a solid color—red, green, or medium blue. The width is determined by the size of the child's hands. Place the child's hands, palms down, on the cloth with the thumbs stretched out and the thumb tips touching. The width of the cloth is measured by the distance between the outside edges of the hands. Have the child extend his or her arms. The length of the cloth is the distance between the outstretched fingertips.

The edges of the cloth should be bound with ½'' bias tape to prevent raveling. The only other accessory for a breechcloth is an ordinary belt. The breechcloth is worn by pulling the front end under the belt and letting it hang down until it nearly reaches the kneecaps; the other end is drawn between the legs, then up in back under the belt, and allowed to hang down nearly to the backs of the knees. Decorate the apron portion of the cloth with tribal designs or symbols of the child's name.

Even five- and six-year-olds can make breechcloths out of muslin to wear in meetings. They can create designs with ordinary crayons, including their own Indian names and the name of the tribe. Lay a piece of waxed paper over the designs and press them in with a hot iron to make them washable. You can also use colorfast magic markers. This is a good beginning costume project.

Armbands

Secure aluminum or leather strips 2'' x 8'' to 10'' (depending on the size of the parent's or child's arm), ½'' wooden beads, copper disk or shell, buckskin thongs, feathers, and steel wool.

Form the band to fit the arm size. Decorate the band with copper disk or shell and punch holes at each end of the band for the buckskin thongs. Paint or burn the tribe's or child's name on the band. If it is aluminum, polish it with steel wool. Add feather fluff if desired or decorate with beads, fringe, bells, or other ornaments. Tie the band on the parent's or child's arm. Armbands can also be made from chamois cloth. You will need small colored glass or plastic beads, small bells, needle and thread, small colored feathers, and a hook and eye. Cut the chamois in strips 1½'' wide. Sew the beads on in Indian designs. You can add feathers in the center as shown in the picture below. Edges A and B are folded back about ¼'' inch and sewn to give the edge a finished appearance. Complete by sewing on bells and hook and eye fasteners.

Name Badge

You will need leather scraps, a ballpoint pen or woodburning tool, scissors, and a safety pin. Make a pattern for your tribal emblem out of cardboard (e.g., arrowhead, tomahawk, animal). Trace the pattern on leather and cut it out. Decorate and put the tribe's or child's name on the badge with either a ballpoint pen or a woodburning tool. Sew the safety pin on the back. You can also cut two slits in the top of the badge and thread a leather thong through them to drape the badge around the neck.

Pendant

Pendants are similar to name badges. To make them you will need modeling clay, a pencil or pointed stick, and a 10-penny nail. Roll the modeling clay until you have a round ball about the size of a large marble. Flatten the ball on a smooth, hard surface such as a kitchen countertop or cutting board. Smooth the edges with a wet finger. Draw an animal head or Indian symbol on the top surface.

When the design is finished, wet the nail, and gently push it through the clay to make a hole for the leather thong to pass through. Let the pendant dry, at least overnight. Paint the pendant with bright colors, if desired. The pendant also can be fired in a kiln to make it stronger.

Rattles

Good rattles can be made out of cow horn, gourd, tin cans, or turtle shell. You will also need 1''-diameter doweling 12'' to 18'' long, one dozen dried peas or small pebbles, leather or other material for covering the rattle, leather thong for lacing, glue, paint, yarn tassels, and feathers. Drill holes in the tin can, gourd, or shell to insert the dowel handle. Insert pebbles or dried peas and the dowel. Glue or lace the cloth or leather rattle covering over the tin can, gourd, or shell. Decorate with paints, tassels, or feathers.

Medicine Bag

American Indians wore medicine bags around their necks to protect themselves against the enemy. The materials needed are a leather circle 5'' in diameter, a leather thong long enough to go around the wearer's neck, and a woodburning tool or leather stamping tools.

Decorate the outer side of the leather circle. Then punch hole evenly around the circle, about 1'' from the center. Thread the leather thong through the holes and tie the two ends together.

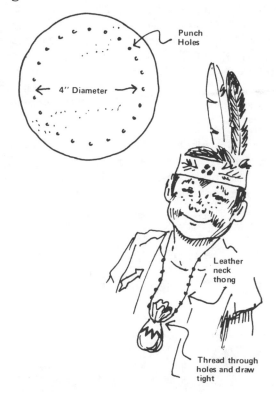

Costume Belt

You can make a decorative belt of leather, plywood, or metal. You will also need twine or a leather thong, paint, and a woodburning tool or metal or leather stamping tools. The material should be cut into enough squares to encircle the wearer's waist. Punch or drill 4 holes in each square. Paint, burn, or stamp a design on each square; then lace them together.

Yarn Anklet

You can do this project at the meeting; it is a quick, easy way to add a decorative touch to costumes. Bring the following materials to the meeting: white yarn cut into 8'' or 9'' strips and one set of shoelaces per child. Give each child one shoestring. Give each parent a handful of yarn strips. While the child holds the string taut, the parent takes each strip of yarn, doubles it, and hangs it over the shoestring.

The yarn is secured to the shoestring by bringing the loose ends through the looped end of the yarn and pulling the yarn taut. Have the child tie the yarn onto the shoestring once he or she sees how to do it. Repeat the process until all the yarn is attached to the shoestring. Make sure you have enough to go around the child's ankle. It will make a feathery-looking anklet.

Indian Dress

This is a project for Princesses and Maidens. The dress requires approximately 3½' x 36'' material, preferably something durable such as bleached muslin, burlap, denim, or sail-

cloth. The material should be twice the length from the wearer's shoulders to her calf or ankle. Choose a bright color like red, blue, or green.

Start by making a pattern from a simple kimono-sleeved dress, or use an extra large paper bag. Cut a hole in the bag large enough to slip over the wearer's head easily; also cut out armholes in the sides of the bag. Check and mark the width of the shoulders for comfort. Add enough width on each side to make the sleeves the desired length. Cut and fit the pattern to the wearer from under the arms to the hemline. All Indian dresses should fit loosely.

Lay the entire pattern out on the full length of the material. Then cut the material 1'' wider than the pattern to allow for seams.

Fold the material at the shoulders and sew the seams on the wrong side. Sew from the end of the sleeves to the hemline on both sides before turning the dress right-side out.

Hem around the neck, sleeves, and bottom of the dress. Sew 6''-long fringe of soft leather, leatherette, or plastic to the bottom of the sleeves and the skirt.

Sew decorated bands to form a triangle on the front of the dress at the neck. If fringe is desired on the decorative bands, sew it on the bands before sewing them on the dress.

Ceremonial Headdresses

These headdresses are elaborate ceremonial costume wear and take work and patience to create. The results, however, can be quite impressive. The instructions on the next page show how to create one, assuming you can find a good supply of natural or artificial feathers.

Lances

With ingenuity and patience, you can make lances that add an authentic touch to ceremonial occasions. The instructions on page 78 show you how to make lances based on the Blackfoot or Sioux pattern. This project can be completed by the entire tribe or assigned to two or three families.

GLUE

FEATHER

FLUFF

GLUE

TAPE

SHOE STRING

FELT

TIE WITH YARN

INSIDE OF FEATHERS

OLD FELT HAT MAKES CROWN

MAJOR PLUME IS A STRIPPED QUILL. 1/2" TO 3/4" WIDTH OF LOOP

1"

FLUFFS

1/2"

BEADED BROWBAND AND ROSETTES

BLACKFOOT PATTERN

Head carved to look like flint -- shaft slotted to take shank of head -- bind with rawhide

8" feathers

Fur

Fur tassels

Bright colors

SIOUX PATTERN

Carved to look like flint or use flat steel

Slot shaft -- insert head and wrap with rawhide

White rabbit fur

8" feathers inserted into sewn slots in bright colored cloth band

Band tied here for gripping point

Lance shaft brightly decorated

6'

Crafts

Craft projects are recommended for tribal meetings and play an important part in the life of every well-organized tribe. As parents and children participate in craft programs, they develop a sense of achievement and pride in their handiwork. Crafts afford children opportunities to

- use their hands to make various items;
- discover new areas of interest and satisfaction;
- share activities with their parents; and
- create items that can be displayed during tribal meetings, in public, or at home.

At the same time, parents have a chance to share their skills with other families, to work closely with their own children, and to tap some new interest or skill areas of their own.

KEY FACTORS IN CRAFT PROGRAMS

Select projects with great care, taking into consideration the children's ages, skills, and development. Start out with simpler projects that younger children can do, then work up to the more difficult crafts as the children's abilities develop. Pay attention to the children's reactions to the project you have selected. The pleasure they take in doing it, and the problems they may have, will indicate whether the next project should be more challenging, more simple, or in a different category. Avoid encouraging competition among the children in making projects. Remember these are projects for both adults and children: Emphasize parent-child teamwork. Finally, vary the types of projects from meeting to meeting.

Advance preparation is the secret to a successful project for the Y-Indian tribal meeting. The attention span of the five- to nine-year-old child is short. Plan projects that are about fifteen minutes long. For the best results, follow these simple guidelines.

- Know the craft well yourself. Complete a sample prior to the meeting so that you know how long the craft takes to make.
- Have all materials ready in advance and separate them into parts for each parent-child team.
- Arrange distribution of materials for a quick start.
- Plan teaching steps carefully, involving all parents and children in the process. Explain the craft as clearly as possible (diagrams sometimes help).
- Be alert to safety factors and group behavior so that no one gets hurt. This is particularly important when using any cutting tools or electrical equipment.
- Allow time to display completed projects if possible and/or help parents and children pack their projects so they arrive home in one piece.
- Make sure that parents and children work together. Be alert for parents who take over their children's tasks in the project or who sit back and let the children do everything.
- Expose the children to a variety of craft media—paint, wood, paper, plastic, clay, leather, metals, plaster of paris, and so on.
- Evaluate the craft program in terms of success and need for improvement.

PROGRESSION IN EXPERIENCE

The skills of parents and children vary widely in any tribe. Five-year-olds need a great deal more help than nine-year-olds, and you will need to adjust the complexity of crafts to the age and skill levels of the children.

For *first-year tribes*, making nameplates and armbands is appropriate. Drawing, painting, and displaying animal, bird, and fish pictures are also feasible. Simplicity is the key.

Second-year tribes likewise need to have simple projects that take a fairly short time to complete. Avoid spending a lot of money on craft materials. Parents' imaginations and good planning will spark some creative ideas for anklets, breechcloths, leaf displays, bird feeders, plywood cutouts of animals, holiday decorations, and beanbag tosses.

Third-year tribes require creativity and a change in craft projects if you want to maintain their interest. Tap the skills and hobbies of the parents. Use authentic American Indian arts and crafts for worthwhile projects. Try new materials besides wood and paper.

In the following sections, we divide the crafts into seven categories: Indian Decorations and Accessories, Holiday Crafts, Household Items, Nature Crafts, Gifts, Games and Toys, and Art. The projects listed in each category vary from simple to complex and should provide hours of fun and a sense of achievement for the parents and children in your tribe.

INDIAN DECORATIONS AND ACCESSORIES

These craft projects enable you to create decorations for your tribal meetings and to add to the costumes of parents and children.

Cut-Straw Necklace

Materials: Plastic straws, scissors, colored yarn or leather thong, masking tape.

Cut plastic straws at various angles and in various lengths. String the cut pieces on colored yarn or a leather thong. To thread the yarn through the straws more easily, wrap a piece of masking tape around one end of the yarn.

Dyed-Macaroni Necklace

Materials: Macaroni, food coloring, waxed dental floss.

Dip pieces of dry (uncooked) macaroni into water tinted with food coloring. After they have absorbed the color, remove and let them dry on a paper towel. String the macaroni on waxed dental floss.

Dried-Vegetable Necklace

Materials: Carrots and potatoes, knife, toothpicks, waxed dental floss, varnish or craft sealer.

Cut carrots and potatoes into chunks. Poke a hold through the center of each chunk with a toothpick and string all the cut vegetables on waxed dental floss. Hang necklace in a cool, dry place for several days. Once the vegetables are dried, they can be varnished or sprayed with sealer.

Indian Necklace

Materials: Bleached chicken bones (leg bones work well), acorns with tight-fitting caps, drill, string or leather thong.

Scrub several chicken bones and leave them for several weeks in a sunny place to bleach. When they are well dried and bleached by the sun, drill holes through one end. Gather acorns with tight caps and drill one hole through the body of each acorn. Starting at the center, alternate acorns and bones as shown in the picture; then string acorns for the rest of the necklace. Tie in back.

Ankle Bells

Materials: 1½'' wide piece of leather or vinyl, hole-punch, leather thong or shoe lace, small bells.

Cut a 1½'' wide strip of leather or vinyl that is the length of the wearer's ankle or upper arm. Punch 4 evenly spaced holds in the strip for the bells and 1 hold at each end. Insert a leather thong or shoelace down through the first hole, up through the second, through a bell, and down through the second hold again. Next, thread the thong up through the third hold, through a bell, and down through the third hole.

Do the same for each hold until all bells are in place and the leather or shoelace comes up through the last hold. Leave the leather or shoelace long enough to tie on the anklet or armband.

Masking Tape Wampum Dish

Materials: Small paper bowl, masking tape, cotton balls, shoe polish (wax or paste), rag.

Cover the small bowl completely with small pieces of masking tape that have been ripped from the roll, not cut. Be sure all edges overlap so that none of the bowl shows through. Dip a cotton ball in shoe polish and rub into the grain of the tape. Pass the wampum dish around at meetings.

Paper Beads

Materials: Colored-print section of the newspaper, glue, toothpicks, leather thong or string, varnish or craft sealer.

Cut triangles about 1½" at the base and 8" on each side from the colored-print section of the newspaper. Apply a few drops of glue to one side of the paper and roll it neatly around the length of a toothpick. Remove the toothpick immediately and let dry. String the beads when you have enough. They can be varnished or sprayed with a craft sealer.

Arrowhead Emblem

Materials: Leather scraps, scissors, hole-punch, plastic thong, woodburning tool or leather working tools.

Cut out a 3" to 4" arrowhead from leather scraps. Punch holes around the edge and inter-

lace with colorful plastic thong. Burn or mark child's name and tribal name on the arrowhead.

Clay Bead Jewelry

Materials: Water-based modeling clay, toothpicks, paints, string or leather thong; varnish (optional).

Roll or press clay into beads of different shapes (squares, balls, diamonds, rectangles, circles, etc.) about 1" thick. Pierce a hole through each one with a toothpick. Remember, clay shrinks when it dries, so the hole must be big enough to thread a string through when the bead is finished. Allow the clay beads to dry thoroughly, then paint them. You can add a final coat of varnish if you wish. String the beads when the paint and/or varnish is dry.

Salt Dough Beads

Materials: Saucepan, flour, salt, water, measuring cup, food coloring, nails, shoelace or leather thong.

In a saucepan, stir together ½ cup of flour, 1 cup of salt, ¼ cup of water, and 3 drops of food coloring.

Cook over medium flame until the dough thickens, then let it cool. When you can hold it in your hands, roll bits of dough into balls and punch a hold through the middle of each with a nail. Let them dry overnight, then string them on a shoelace or leather thong. You can make several batches of dough in different colors, and your beads can be many different shapes.

Dance Rattle

Materials: Stick 12" to 18" long, about 20 bottle caps, a ball of string, 20 pieces of string cut into 4" or 5" lengths, glue, brightly colored feathers, paint, punching tool.

Punch a hole in the center of each bottle cap. On one end of each piece of 4" to 5" string, tie a knot. Tie string through the bottom of the cap. Tie a knot in the string about 1" higher and add another cap.

Paint the stick with glue and wrap with string, starting at the bottom. About halfway up the stick, lay the short strings with the bottle caps over the stick and wrap the long string around them to hold them in place. Make sure the strings with the bottle caps are evenly spaced, as shown in the picture.

At the top of the stick, glue on some brightly colored feathers and wrap them securely with the string. Paint the stick.

Deerskin

Materials: Grocery bags or brown mural paper, crayons (or markers, water colors, etc.), tape.

Have each parent-child team draw the shape of a deerskin on a large piece of brown mural paper or opened-out grocery bag (you can find pictures of deerskins in library books). Have each parent-child team draw symbols, objects, people, ideas, or anything else on the deerskin with crayons. Ask each pair to tape its deerskin to the wall and explain what the pictures mean.

You can also do this project on pieces of leather, as long as you can purchase the leather at a reasonable cost. This material is more permanent and can be kept as a record of a trip, council, or other memorable event in the life of the tribe or of a particular parent-child team.

Tepee

Materials: 5 pieces of cardboard, 55" × 25" wide at the base × 5" wide at the top; paints; yarn (leather thongs or shoelaces work as well); punching tool.

Cut a 20" long door that is 18" wide at the bottom and 11" wide at the top out of one of the pieces of cardboard. Decorate each piece with Indian designs, the tribal name, events from tribal activities, and so forth. Punch holes in the edge of the cardboard pieces and tie the 5 pieces together with 10" pieces of yarn, leather thong, shoelace, or other strong material.

Navajo Bread

Materials: An electric fry pan, large and small mixing bowls, mixing spoons, measuring spoons, rubber spatula, measuring cup, egg beater, small platter or tray. *Ingredients:* Corn oil, dry yeast, water, eggs, salt, flour, honey.

Measure 6 cups of flour into a large bowl. Measure 2 cups lukewarm water (100°F) into a small bowl. Add 1 tablespoon salt, ¼ cup honey, ¼ cup corn oil, and one envelope of dry yeast. When yeast is thoroughly dissolved, add 1 beaten egg to liquid mixture. Pour this mixture into 6 cups flour in the large bowl. Mix. Knead by turning bowl with left hand and manipulating dough with the right hand.

At the end of 8 to 10 minutes of kneading, you will have a ball of dough weighing about 56 ounces. It should be smooth and elastic. Divide the bread into 1½-ounce pieces (about ¼ cup) and, with your thumbs, shape each

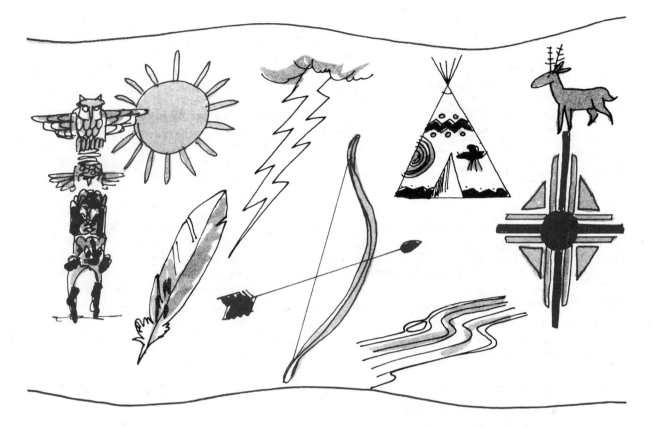

piece into a flat circle, about 4'' or 5'' in diameter.

Pour corn oil into the electric fry pan and heat to 375°. Once the oil is well heated, place 4 circles of bread at a time into the hot oil. Fry until golden brown, then turn and brown the other side. Add more oil each time you fry another batch. Butter each piece while it's hot.

To store the bread, put it in a plastic bag in the freezer. When you want a piece, take one out, put in the toaster, and eat it while it's piping hot. Yield: about 38 pieces.

Story Mural

Materials: Newsprint, markers or crayons, brown mural paper, tape.

This project requires two meetings to complete. At the first meeting, use the newsprint to record ideas generated by a group discussion on the group's purpose, history, background, and members. Discuss what the members know about the Indians for whom the tribe is named. Brainstorm as many ideas about the identity of your group as you can and list them on the newsprint.

At the next meeting, explain that you as a group will be creating a story mural using ideas brainstormed at the previous meeting. (Make sure you have the newsprint from that meeting on hand.) You might point out that what you are creating is much like the American Indian wall designs. Roll out the brown mural paper so that every parent-child team has some space on which to draw. Decide who will draw which part and begin.

You can take the mural with you on campouts and from meeting to meeting; you can even add to it as your tribal history continues.

HOLIDAY CRAFTS

Holiday crafts are especially popular with young children. These projects give them a chance to learn new skills and to create thoughtful gifts or decorations for others.

Jack-O'-Lanterns

Materials: Pumpkins, carving knives, jackknives, spoons for scooping out pumpkin seeds, candles, newspaper.

If the tribal meeting falls in October, carving pumpkins for Halloween is lots of fun despite the mess involved. Parents will need to help the children with doing the artwork, carving, and placing the candle. Spread newspaper to make cleanup easier.

Halloween Spiders

Materials: Large black pom-pom, three 4'' black chenille stems, glue, plastic eyes, elastic thread. Another type of spider will require a large wooden bead, three 6'' black chenille stems, paints, paint brush.

To make the pom-pom spider, glue the sticks to the bottom of the pom-pom and bend for legs. Add plastic eyes and tie elastic thread around the pom-pom so the spider bounces when hanging.

To make the bead spider, select a wooden bead with a hole big enough to pass through the 3 chenille sticks. Bend stick ends to form 6 legs. Paint eyes on the bead and use elastic thread to suspend the spider from the ceiling.

Sour Ball Ornaments

Materials: 5 unwrapped sour ball candies, 1 muffin tin, oil, string.

Place 5 unwrapped sour ball candies in each section of a lightly greased muffin tin. Bake in a 375° oven for 6-8 minutes, being careful not to let the candy bubble and turn brittle. Remove from oven and immediately poke a hanging hole at the top of each candy ornament with a wet toothpick (not too close to the edge). When the candies have cooled, invert the pan and pop them out by pressing on the back of each muffin well. String the candies and hang them on a tree or in the window.

Coffee Can Luminaria

Materials: A 1- or 2-pound coffee can, pencils, brown paper, tape, pencil, various sizes of nails, hammer, spray paint, candles.

This project is perfect for winter holidays. Fill a 1- or 2-pound coffee can with water and freeze it solid. Cut a piece of brown paper to fit perfectly around the outside of the can. Lay the paper out flat and draw a design on it, preferably something simple; then secure it around the can. Using various sizes of nails, punch holes in the can to outline the design. Remove the paper and let the ice melt so that you can pour out the water. Spray paint the outside of the can and, when dry, place a candle inside. The flame will illuminate the punched design.

Christmas Angels

Materials: Disposable aluminum pie plates, stapler or paper clips, pencil (optional).

Cut out the bottom of the pie plate. On half of the circle, cut out an angel pattern (see illustration). Bend the halo and the wings forward. Roll the body of the angel into a cone shape. Fasten the back with a stapler or paper clip. If you are using the angels for invitations, print your message with a dull pencil before you roll the body into a cone. This imprints the lettering into the aluminum.

Christmas Ornaments

Materials: Aluminum frozen food plates, brightly colored wrapping or construction paper, stapler, hole-punch, string or ribbon, scissors.

Have everyone save aluminum frozen food plates and bring as many as possible to the meeting. You will also need some brightly colored paper—Christmas wrapping paper or construction paper will do. Cut out 2 circles

of aluminum and 1 of colored paper, all the same size. Put the paper between the aluminum like a sandwich. Staple all 3 together on the center line (see illustration). Bend the aluminum flaps so the color will show. Punch a hole at the top for a string and hang the decoration on your tree. Try other shapes such as diamonds, squares, and triangles.

Christmas Garlands

Materials: Popped popcorn, cranberries, macaroni, construction paper, aluminum frozen food plates, scissors, large darning needle, heavy thread.

Your tribe can make garlands and chains to go on your tree. Prepare a bowl of popcorn, and buy fresh cranberries and a box of macaroni. Cut some small circles from colored con-

struction paper and aluminum frozen food plates. String the various items on the thread to make a gay and colorful chain or garland to hang on the tree.

String Ornaments

Materials: Balloons, household string, white glue, spray paint, ribbons, newspaper.

Ordinary household string wound around small balloons makes a lovely ornament. Inflate each balloon. Soak the string in white glue, then wrap around the balloon. Hang the balloon over newspaper or other covered surface while drying. When the string is dry, prick the balloon and remove it. Spray paint the resulting ornament, and tie or glue a ribbon on the top as a hanger.

Decorated Glue Disks

Materials: Lightweight cardboard, white glue, aluminum foil, dried corn (or cloves, peppercorns, etc.), food coloring, small paper cups, tweezers, toothpicks, assorted ribbons, nylon fishing line.

Glue disks can be decorated with corn, spices, or food coloring; they make attractive ornaments. Cut strips from cardboard ½" wide and 8"-11" long. Glue the ends of each strip together so that each forms a circle. Let dry, then shape to make the circle completely round. Lay circles on aluminum foil and pour in glue. Spread with a toothpick, making sure the glue touches the cardboard all the way around.

You create the spice ornament before the glue has dried. With the tweezers, arrange spices to look like a flower. Press in place, dry.

For the painted designs, mix glue with food coloring. Use separate paper cups to mix colors. When glue circles are completely dry, lightly draw in designs, following your own or tracing from greeting cards or coloring books. Fill in the designs with glue-paint—using one color at a time and letting each one dry before applying the next. Glue-paint is applied by pouring a few drops, then spreading with toothpicks.

To complete ornaments, lift from foil and glue ribbon around cardboard circles and a flat ribbon bow on top. Tie with fishing line for hanging.

Light Bulb Snowman

Materials: Used light bulb, Styrofoam ball, black and red construction paper or felt, jar lid, plaster of paris, white tempera paint, paint brush, glue.

Paint light bulb with white tempera paint. When paint is dry, glue the Styrofoam ball on the tapered bulb end for the snowman's head. It may be necessary to scoop out a bit of the ball so it will fit. Mix plaster of paris and pour into jar lid. As it begins to set, stand light bulb on it and hold until firm. Cut hat from black paper or felt and glue to head. Cut features from black paper or felt and glue to face. Cut scarf from red paper or felt and glue around neck. Try this same idea for other holiday figures such as Santa, pilgrims, ghosts, and the like.

Clothespin Reindeer

Materials: 3 flattop clothespins, 2 plastic circles for eyes, red and green felt scraps, nylon fishing line, glue; stain, white felt scraps, tiny bell, gold thread (optional).

If you wish to stain clothespins, do so ahead of time so they have a chance to dry thoroughly. For the reindeer body, glue 2 clothespins together. Glue a third one with open end pointing up, but make sure the groove on the side of all the clothespins lines up, as shown in the picture. Glue on nose of red felt, plastic eyes, and holly antlers made out of green felt. You can add a white felt tail and tiny bell on a gold thread around the neck.

Crystal Icicle

Materials: 6'' white chenille stem, 5 crystal paddle wheel beads, 11 crystal tri-beads, four 10-mm multifaceted crystal beads, four 6-mm multifaceted crystal beads, nylon fishing line.

Loop and knot nylon fishing line to make a hanger for the icicle. Bend and crimp one end of the chenille stick over the center of the hanger. Thread the beads onto the chenille stick from the bottom in this order: all paddle wheels, all tri-beads, all large multifaceted beads, all small multifaceted beads. Bend the bottom end of the chenille stick snugly around the last bead to finish the ornament.

Cylinder Cardholder

Materials: 1 large can (2-pound coffee can or potato chip can), yarn.

Remove the top and bottom lids from the can. Drop one end of the yarn through the can, bring it up on the outside, and tie it so that it forms a snugly fitting loop. Pull the knot around so that it is on the inside of the can. Continue to tie loops around the can, remembering to pull tightly as you go. Fit each strand snugly to the one before it so that none of the container shows through. Slide a Christmas card onto the strands so that each strand fits in the fold of the card. If a card is too tall, trim it down so that it fits on the can.

Novelty Candles

Materials: Molds, wax, wicks, color (crayon pieces), double boiler or 1-pound coffee can and saucepan, match (or nail, pencil, or piece of wood or metal).

The most important part of the candle is the wick. Single strand ordinary string does not burn correctly. For home candlemaking, buy wicks from a craft supply store, melt down cheap candles, or braid string. Molds may be tin cans, dessert molds, muffin tins, cardboard milk containers, wet sand, or anything that will contain hot wax. Using a real wick, you can make adequate candles from ordinary paraffin wax. For slower burning candles, add to the paraffin approximately 20 percent stearic acid and 5-10 percent beeswax, found in drugstores or craft stores. Color the wax by adding pieces of crayons.

After you choose the mold, melt the wax in a double boiler over a slow fire. A 1-pound coffee can may be placed inside another pan with water in it to make a double boiler. Bend the can to make a spout. To hold the wick in the center of the mold while pouring, tie one end of it to a match, nail, pencil, or piece of wood or metal and set it over the edge so the wick hangs straight down in the mold. Let the wax harden thoroughly, then remove from the mold.

HOUSEHOLD ITEMS

Projects to make household items give parents and children an opportunity to make practical, useful objects that contribute to family life. Children particularly enjoy making things that other family members use and value.

Napkin Rings

Materials: Cardboard tube, scissors, glue, yarn (or braid or rick-rack).

A paper towel or toilet paper cardboard tube works well for this project. Slice the tube into 1" lengths to make the napkin ring base. Glue one end of the yarn, braid, or rick-rack to the inside of the ring. Loop the material around the ring until the entire surface is covered. Make enough rings for everyone in the family plus 2 or 3 guests.

Windproof Napkin Holder

Materials: 1-gallon bleach bottle, knife, stapler, coat hanger, wire cutter, glue, beads.

Cut the bleach bottle as shown in the picture, removing the top as well. Cut a slot, ⅛" wide, down each side, starting about 2" from the top. Staple the ends together at the top, covering the staple with a 4" flower cut from bottle scraps. To make the bar that holds the napkins in place, cut an 8" length of coat hanger wire. Glue a bead at each end of the wire. Place napkins inside the holder and lay the wire on top of them to keep them in place on windy days.

Camp Pillowcase

Materials: Carbon or dressmaker's paper, plain pillowcase, ballpoint tube paints or colorfast magic markers.

Using carbon or dressmaker's paper, trace a design, name, or picture onto a plain pillowcase. Paint the picture with ballpoint tube paints or colorfast magic markers. Allow the paints to dry for 1-2 days before washing the pillowcase.

Dishcloth Placemats

Materials: Dishcloths, large blunt plastic needle, colored yarn.

Reproduce the woven design of the dishcloth by running pieces of yarn in and out of the fabric. Use the large, blunt plastic needle to weave the yarn. The yarn does not need to be secured but can extend 3" to 4" on either side as fringe.

Decorated Soap Dish

Materials: Plastic soap dish, acrylic or ball-point tube paints.

Use the paints to decorate a plain plastic soap dish with designs, patterns, pictures, or names.

Furry Refrigerator Magnets

Materials: Drinking glass, scissors or art knife, fake fur, magnetic tape strip, small pom-pom, wiggle eyes.

Trace the rim of a drinking glass on the back side of a piece of fake fur. Cut it out, being careful not to cut through the fur but just the backing. Brush the fur outward. Glue the pom-pom nose and wiggle eyes in the center. Apply magnetic tape strip to back after removing adhesive backing.

Plaster of Paris Refrigerator Magnets

Materials: Plaster of paris, plastic bottle caps (1⅞" in diameter), emery board or sandpaper, paints, paint brush, decals, magnetic tape strip, scissors, petroleum jelly.

Mix plaster of paris according to directions. If exact proportions are not available, use 1 part water to 2 parts plaster. Add the plaster to the water and mix until smooth. It sets quickly, so make a small batch at a time.

Lightly coat the plastic caps with petroleum jelly and pour the plaster into them. Do not make them too thick or the magnetic tape will not hold them onto the refrigerator. After the plaster has dried, remove it from the plastic caps and sand the edges smooth. Paint the circles after they are *absolutely* dry. Apply the decals at this time as well. Then cut a piece of magnetic tape, remove pull-off adhesive backing, and stick on the back.

Alternative: Use metal cookie cutters for molds and make Christmas tree ornaments. Pour plaster about ¼" thick. Place molds on a surface covered with foil or waxed paper. If they do not rest flat, place a weight on top. Make a hole for the hanger before plaster is completely set. Use a toothpick or small nail, but don't leave it in the plaster or you won't be able to pull it out.

Refrigerator Decorations

Materials: Coloring book, scissors, sheets of art foam, sequins, braid, trim, glitter, markers, magnetic tape strip.

Art foam comes in an assortment of colors. Children's coloring books offer simple and good-sized patterns. Cut out the patterns and glue them onto the foam. Trim the designs with glitter, trim, sequins, and braid. Draw features or other detail with markers. Cut and fix piece of magnetic tape to back.

Drinking Glasses

Materials: Jelly glasses, paper, pencil, enamel paints, tape, brush.

Draw a design on a piece of paper that will fit inside the jelly glass. Tape the picture in place so it can be seen from the outside. Paint the design on the outside of the glass with colorful enamels. Place the glass on a cookie sheet and put into a 225° oven for 20 minutes.

Birch Mementos

Materials: Length of white birch 4" to 6" in diameter, ring or other type of hanger, woodburning or woodcarving tools or paints and paint brush, natural materials (pinecones, fungi, shells), varnish.

Slice the white birch diagonally into ½"-thick slabs, like a loaf of bread. Parents with power tools can do this easily or you can ask the local lumberyard operator to slice the wood. Decorate the slabs with woodburned, carved, or painted designs or use natural materials such as pinecones, fungi, or shells. Complete the project with a ring at the top (or other device for hanging) and a coat of varnish.

Bookmarker

Materials: 1½" x 10" leather, paper, or cloth strips; pencil; paint or leatherworking tools.

Draw a design on the surface of the material, then paint the design or use leatherworking tools if you are working with leather. Personalize the design with something that has meaning to both parent and child.

Shoeshine Kit

Materials: 3 pieces of ¼" plywood for bottom and side pieces, 3 pieces of ¾" pine board (2 for ends and 1 for handle), sandpaper, hammer, nails, glue.

Cut out plywood pieces before the meeting, as shown in the picture. Sand the rough edges. Assemble the pieces with glue and nails. Have parents and children take their unfinished kits home to paint or varnish them.

Tie Rack

Materials: ½" plywood or composition board, ¼" dowel and small cleats (or metal crossbar), hammer, nails, decals or paints and paint brush, varnish.

Cut out plywood before the meeting, as shown in the diagram. Attach dowel with small cleats or use a purchased metal rack crossbar. Paint or apply decals for an artistic finish. Varnish finished project.

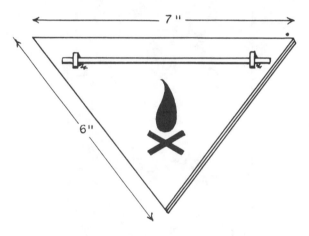

Windmill or Weather Vane

Materials: Stiff paper, 18" stick or dowel, scissors, knife, nails, hammer, glue, mounting stick.

Cut out a paper propeller from stiff paper and a triangle with rounded corners for the tail piece. Nail the paper propeller onto one end of the dowel so that the propeller spins freely.

Cut a slit in the other end of the dowel and insert the paper triangle, securing it with glue or a nail. Nail the dowel to the mounting stick so that it swings freely with a change in wind direction.

Clay Bowl or Jar

Materials: Water-base clay, pictures of Indian bowls, sticks or other tools for drawing designs in clay, paints and paint brush.

Secure water-base clay from your hobby or craft store. Ask for clay that does not need to be kiln-fired in order to harden. Mold the clay into bowls, following pictures you have gathered of Indian bowls. Use sticks or other objects with various blunt, pointed, or flat ends to etch designs into the wet clay. Place the bowls in a sunny or warm place until they are thoroughly dry and hard. Paint Indian designs around the sides.

Paper Pottery

Materials: Paper rolls, white glue, scissors, tape, paints and paint brush or markers.

Paper pottery, created with paper and glue, can look very much like clay products. Start with a roll of paper. The size of the roll will determine the type of shapes you can make. A thick but small-diameter paper roll can make a bud vase; a thick, large-diameter paper roll can make a bowl.

Ready-made rolls are easy to find. Just purchase adding machine or cash register tapes or shelf paper rolls. If the rolls are wound too tightly to press out the center with your thumbs, you may have to unwind and rewind them more loosely. If the paper roll is too thick, cut it down by unwinding it to the proper size and cutting off the excess paper.

You may also want to make your own paper rolls. To do so, cut even strips of paper from newspaper, a paper pad, or typing paper. Slightly overlap the strips and tape or glue them end to end. Wind the paper strip to make a spiral roll and tape the end so the roll won't unravel.

To make the pottery, press the center of the roll out with your thumbs and fingers, and ease the sides up and out. Don't go up too far or the whole form may fall apart.

When you have created the shape, mix a small cup of white glue with a little water. Spread the glue evenly with your finger or a paint brush over the entire surface, inside and out. When the glue has dried, paint the pottery as you wish.

Corn Planter

Materials: Wide-mouth jar, pebbles, loose earth, a packet of corn or bean seeds.

First put about ½" of pebbles in the bottom of the jar (a peanut butter jar works well). Add about 2" of loose earth. Plant 5 or 6 corn or bean seeds about ½" deep where they can be seen through the sides of the jar. Water them according to instructions on the packet. Soon you will be able to see the tiny roots grow out of the seeds. As they grow larger, you may want to transplant them to a larger pot or to a garden outside.

Pellon Banner

Materials: Pellon (5 yards cut into 10" x 12" pieces), 12" long wood dowels, black and red marking pens, patterns, stapler or glue, crayons, yarn; sequins and glitter, pencil, paper (optional).

Cut pellon into 10" x 12" pieces before the meeting. Select a pattern and trace the picture onto the pellon with a marking pen. Fill in the picture with crayons, pressing hard for a more brilliant effect. Staple or glue the banner onto the dowel. Tie yarn to the dowel to hang the banner. You can also add decorative touches by putting fringe on the bottom or gluing sequins and glitter on the material. If the children wish to draw their own designs, suggest that they draw them first on paper and then trace the patterns onto the pellon.

Wind Chimes

Materials: 3 clay pots (3" in diameter), 1 yard of heavy macrame cord, 3 ceramic beads (1" in diameter), acrylic paints and paint brush; drill (optional).

Paint the pots with colorful designs. If pots do not have drainage holes, drill holes in the center of the bottom of each pot. Make a hanging loop in one end of the macrame cord. Slide 1 pot up the cord to within 10" of the loop and make a knot on the inside of the pot to hold it in place. Slide 1 of the ceramic beads up the cord until it is just inside the rim of the pot. Tie a knot to hold it in place. Repeat with 2 other pots and beads, leaving a 10" space between each pot. Hang the wind chime in a place where it will sway in the wind. The ceramic beads will strike the sides of the pot and create a soft, ringing sound.

Old-Key Wind Chimes

Materials: Tin can rim or metal ring, yarn or twine to cover rim, nylon fishing line, old keys.

Wrap a tin can rim with yarn or twine to cover the metal surface. (To remove rim, place it into the can opener head on after removing top.) Tie varying lengths of nylon fishing line through holes in keys. Tie opposite ends of lines to metal ring. Keys should be grouped in 3s or 4s at 1 or 2 different levels so they will touch each other at the slightest breeze or movement. Tie 4 more strands of fishing line to the ring at evenly spaced intervals. Holding the ring in the air, pull the ends of the strands together above it and tie them in an overhand knot. The ring should hang straight.

Kitchen Wreath

Materials: Heavy cardboard or Styrofoam wreath; brown florist's tape; various spices, beans, dried peas, popcorn, birdseed; spaghetti; glue; spray varnish; hanger; ribbon and bow.

Cut small wreath shape (7" diameter) from double thickness of heavy cardboard or purchase a small Styrofoam wreath. Wrap completely with brown florist's tape. Gather various kitchen spices and dried seeds, pop-

corn, birdseed, and the like. Determine how many sections you want on your wreath, and mark them by gluing 2 pieces of spaghetti on the wreath to make the divisions. Glue different arrangements of spices and seeds into each section until the wreath is completely covered.

When the glue dries, spray on varnish for shine. Glue hanger on the back of the wreath and add a bow or ribbon around the outside edge.

Carryalls From Soda Pop Cartons

Materials: One 6- or 8-pack soda pop container, art knife, paints and paint brush, decorations or wallpaper scraps, glue, small fruit cans (for tool carryall).

This project can be made to carry household items or tools. For household items, paint the carton and remove the dividers on one side. Finish the outside by painting on your own decorations or gluing on cutouts from magazines, wallpaper scraps, and so on. Use the open side for carrying paper plates and napkins and the other side for silverware and condiments.

To make a tool carryall, follow the same steps as above, but, instead of removing dividers, insert small painted fruit cans into each section. Use these cans to hold screwdrivers, pliers, and the like.

Sunburst Hot Pad or Wall Decoration

Materials: 39 popsicle sticks, 39 wooden beads (⅜" in diameter), ⅜"-diameter heavy-duty string or thread, 6" ruler, pliers, ³⁄₃₂"-diameter drill, large blunt needle, scissors.

Drill 2 holes in each popsicle stick (see illustration). Thread the needle with the string, then use the needle to thread the end hole of all 39 sticks. Tighten the string as much as you can and make one loop of a square knot. Have someone hold the loop tightly with pliers. Finish the knot and clip the ends.

String the wooden beads at the second hole, alternating sticks and beads until you have 39 of each to form a circular design. Tighten the string so that the mat lies flat and knot the thread. Clip the ends to finish the sunburst hot pad or wall decoration.

NATURE CRAFTS

Nature craft projects provide hours of fun and enrich parents' and children's appreciation of the natural beauty around them. Hikes, fishing trips, boat trips, and camp-outs provide many opportunities to collect natural objects and observe nature. These projects emphasize using what is available in nature and adding only a minimum of ready-made materials.

Animal Tracks

Materials: Plaster of paris, knife, pencil, plywood plaque, screws or glue (optional).

This craft project provides multiple learning opportunities. You can take a trip to the forest or beach to discover wild animal or bird tracks. Of course, you can also look for dog, cat, and squirrel prints closer to home.

When you find a set of clear prints, mix the plaster of paris in a container, stirring it to a smooth, spreadable consistency. Pour mixture into the animal track, and let it dry for 20 minutes before lifting. Trim the plaster with a knife to remove excess matter; then label the mold with the name of the animal that made the track. Later, you might want to add the place where the track was found, the date it was found, and other information about the animal. You may want to mount the plaster cast on a plywood plaque with glue or screws.

Pinecone Bird Feeder

Materials: Large pinecone, peanut butter, birdseed, string.

Tie a string on the pinecone for hanging. Then cover the pinecone with peanut butter and roll it in birdseed. Hang it up in a tree.

Corn Cob Bird Feeder

Materials: 4 corn cobs, 4 large spikes, 2 sticks, nails, hammer.

Drive the large spikes through 1 stick at equal intervals. Stick a corn cob on each spike. Nail this stick to the top of the other one in the shape of a "T." Post the bird feeder in the ground and watch the birds come.

Coat Hanger Bird Feeder

Materials: Coffee can, 2 pie tins, coat hanger, can opener, nail, hammer, wire cutters, dark paint, paint brush, rubber tubing (optional).

Cut a row of "V"-shaped openings around the open end of the coffee can. Punch nail holes in both pie tins and through the closed end of the can as shown in the illustration. Cut the coat hanger in the center of the bottom wire and put ends through first pie tin, can, and second pie tin as in the illustration. Twist the ends to hold the bird feeder parts tightly together.

If you use aluminum pie tins, thread the coat hanger up over the outside of the can and through the "V"-shaped openings before passing it through the bottom pie tin.

Paint the can a dull color to avoid frightening the birds. You may want to place a piece of rubber hose around the wire that rubs against the tree limb to protect the bark.

When you fill the bird feeder with seeds and hang it on a tree limb, the seed will automatically feed through the "V"-shaped openings.

Suet Log Bird Feeder

Materials: Log that is 1-3' high and at least 6" in diameter, suet, grain, large bore drill, large eye screw, thong or wire.

This is an easy nature project. Make holes in the small log. Fill the holes with melted suet mixed with various grains. Attach a screw with an eye to one end of the log and thread a thong or wire through it to hang the log.

Weed Creatures

Materials: Dried weeds/pods, driftwood or smooth rock, paints and paint brush, decorative materials (wiggle eyes, feathers, pipe cleaners), glue.

Glue dried weeds and/or pods to driftwood or smooth rock in the shape of various creatures. Add features such as painted faces, wiggle eyes, tails, and feathers.

Alternative: Use pinecones as the base for the creatures' bodies. Fashion woodland creatures from a combination of pinecones, small shells, beans, pods, seeds, fungi, feathers, and other natural materials. Use quick-drying glue or cement (such as tacky glue or epoxy) to fix the materials together. Pipe cleaners can serve as legs and necks.

Compact Campfire

Materials: 1 tuna can, cardboard, tin can and saucepan for heating, bar of wax, cardboard, 1 wick.

Line the tuna can with a cardboard strip. Set the wick in the middle of the can. Heat the wax in an old tin can set in a saucepan half filled with water; pour melted wax over cardboard and wick, filling the tuna can to the top. Allow wax to cool. The campfire is ready to warm coffee, cocoa, or food. Handy to have on the trail.

Leaf Plaster Molds

Materials: Plaster of paris, aluminum pie tins, petroleum jelly or vegetable oil, leaves, pencil.

Mix the plaster of paris. Cover each leaf with petroleum jelly or oil and lay it in the bottom of a pie tin, making sure the leaf is lying flat with no bulges or air pockets around the edges. Don't let the plaster get under the leaf or it will be hard to remove from the plaster when dry.

Pour the plaster into each pie tin. Be sure not to make the mold too thick—about ½" to ¾" is fine. Allow the plaster to dry thoroughly before removing from the pie tin. The leaf should peel off, leaving a fine impression in the plaster. Label each mold with the name of the tree and the date the mold was cast.

Mystery Propeller

Materials: 10" stick; small shingle nail; wood (or plastic or aluminum) propeller ⅛"

thick, ½" wide, 2¼" long; a rubbing tool stick or old ballpoint pen; file, saw, or knife; drill.

Notch the 10" stick as shown with a file, saw, or knife, making it ⅛" wide at the top. Drill a hole in the end of the stick for the shingle nail to prevent splitting; attach the propeller with the shingle nail.

Rub the notched stick back and forth vigorously with the rubbing tool and watch the propeller. The propeller can also change directions.

Hummer Button

Materials: 2" wooden disk or large button, heavy string, short sticks for handles, drill.

Drill 2 holes in the wooden disk (or use button) and thread heavy string through the holes. Fasten each end of the string to wooden handles. Pull back and forth to make the disk hum.

Hummer Paddle

Materials: 1 strip of wood ¼" x 1½" wide x 8" long, 1 dowel ½" diameter and 8" long, string, drill.

Drill a hole in one end of the paddle wood and tie it to the dowel, leaving about 1' of slack between the two. Grasp the dowel and swing the paddle vigorously in a circle; listen to it hum.

Terrarium

Materials: 2-liter plastic soda bottle, small plants, potting soil, small stones, small figurines, colored gravel, scissors.

Pry the black plastic bottom carefully from the empty 2-liter bottle. With sharp scissors, cut off the top of the bottle at the neck where it starts to narrow. Fill the black base with potting soil, several small plants, and so forth. If there is any glue remaining on the clear portion of the bottle, run hot tap water over it and the glue will peel off. Attach the clear dome of the bottle to the black bottom. Water your terrarium and set it in a warm place.

Waterscope

Materials: Large tin can, clear plastic bag, heavy rubber band, can opener, tape.

Cut top and bottom from can, and slip the plastic bag over one end. Hold the bag in place with a heavy rubber band. Tape the other end, which is used as the viewing edge, for safety. Hold the covered end underwater and look into the open end.

Crystal Jewels

Materials: 1 ounce of alum, 1 measuring cup, spoon, large jar, saucepan, glass or plastic funnel, cotton or clean cheesecloth, shallow dish, glass jar of alcohol or cleaning fluid or plastic box with cotton covering the bottom.

Put alum in a large jar. Add 1 cup of water and stir. Most of the alum will dissolve. Place the jar in a saucepan ⅓-full of water and heat it slowly over *low* heat. This dissolves the remaining alum in the jar.

When the chemical is completely dissolved, set the jar in a cool place where it is protected from dust and will not be disturbed. Slow cooling forms better crystals.

When the crystals have formed, pour off the remaining solution *slowly* through a filter so that it just drips through into a shallow dish. To make the filter, stuff cotton or cheesecloth into the mouth of a glass or plastic funnel so the liquid will drip through.

Pick out one of the larger, well-shaped crystals remaining in the jar. Place it in the dish containing the solution. The crystal will grow larger as the solution evaporates.

Store the finished crystals in a glass jar of alcohol or cleaning fluid or on a cotton ball in a plastic box.

Natural Window Hanging

Materials: Cardboard furnace filter, clear plastic Contact paper, scissors, wildflowers, tiny leaves and seeds, nylon fishing line.

Cut a piece of furnace filter into desired shape. Lay the piece onto the sticky side of a piece of clear plastic Contact paper. Place 1 leaf, flower, or other decoration in the center of each space in the filter. Lay another piece of Contact paper over this, sticky side in. Trim off excess paper neatly around the edges. Make a small hole at the top for a fishing line hanger.

Dried Food Picture

Materials: Poster board cut into 4" x 6" or 5" x 7" pieces; white glue; pencils; paints and paint brush; dried food such as peas, popcorn, beans, tea leaves, sesame seeds, sunflower seeds, and powdered spices; hanger. (Each parent-child team should bring 2 or 3 dried foods.)

Draw a picture with pencil on a poster board—a tribal scene, a landscape, a series of designs or Indian symbols, animal pictures, or something each parent and child have done together. Paint any background work first; then, working on one section of the picture at a time, outline and fill in your designs or picture by glueing on dried foods. Attach a hanger to the back of the picture.

Rubbish Monster

Materials: Litter, glue, tape, paints and paint brush or markers.

This craft is a good ecology lesson. Ask everyone to bring some rubbish from home or collect litter on a tribal hike and use the materials for this project.

Assemble a monster using a large carton for its body and assorted cans for its arms and legs. Think of additional ways to decorate the monster by adding egg cartons, meat trays, pie tins, bottle caps, lids, and so on. When the monster is complete, put an environmental message on it with paint or markers.

 # GIFTS

The crafts in this section are ideal for birthday or holiday gifts or as tokens of appreciation for people to whom parents and/or children feel especially close. Children can learn the value of showing their gratitude or affection for others in ways that also allow them to develop self-expression and new skills. The projects suggested below range from simple, easy-to-make items to more complicated gifts.

Ribbon Bookmarker

Materials: 2 large wooden beads, 15'' piece of ¾''-wide velvet ribbon, sequins or small glass beads (optional).

Tie a knot about 2'' from each end of the ribbon. Make the knots large enough so the wooden beads will not slide over them. Thread the beads onto the velvet and tie a knot at each end of the ribbon to hold the beads in place. Decorate by sewing sequins or glass beads on the velvet. This project makes a great stocking-stuffer at Christmas.

Felt Bookmarkers

Materials: 9" x 12" felt, scissors, paper pattern, pencil, glue, material scraps.

Select a pattern for the bookmarker, such as those shown in the illustration. The pattern should be about 2-3" wide, so you can make 3 bookmarkers from 1 piece of felt. You should provide paper patterns for the craft or have the parent-child teams make them before the meeting.

Place the paper pattern on the felt and trace around it with a pencil. Cut out the pattern. Repeat the process for the remaining 2 bookmarkers, using the same or a different pattern. Decorate the bookmarkers with scraps of felt or other material, adding eyes, spots, strips, names, and so forth. You can also fringe the ends by making cuts ¼" wide and about 1" long in the felt.

Clay Pencil Holder

Materials: Water-base clay, pencil, tempera paints and paint brush.

Mix the clay according to directions—make sure it does not have to be fired in a kiln. Roll the clay between your hands into a ball about the size of an orange. Whack it down on your worktable to flatten the bottom.

Using a pencil, press 5 or 6 holes about 1" deep and ¾" apart into the clay. Make the holes near the top end of the clay. Widen the holes slightly because the clay often shrinks when it dries.

Carve or cut designs into the clay base with a stick, pencil, or other tool. Allow the clay to dry thoroughly and paint with tempera paints.

Bookworm Pencil

Materials: Pencil, 15" colored pipe cleaner, glue, wiggle eyes, small plastic hat.

Wind the pipe cleaner tightly around the end of the pencil. Glue wiggle eyes and the small plastic hat to the end of the coil to make the bookworm.

Frustration Pencil

Materials: Pencil, craft fur (1" x 3"), small plastic eyes, 10" length of yarn, red felt (circles cut with paper punch for mouth), glue.

When things make you nervous and upset
And you're so frustrated you don't know
*   what to do,*
Just twist this pencil between your palms
And let it blow its top for you!

Part the craft fur before cutting so you can keep the long strands. Wrap fur tightly around pencil, glueing as you go. Leave eraser exposed so it can still be used. Tie securely at neckline with yarn. Glue on eyes and mouth. Stroke fur upwards and follow poem. Include a copy of the poem when you give the pencil to someone.

Clothespin Key Chain

Materials: Wooden clothespin, fine sandpaper, paints and paint brush or markers, screw eye hook, key ring, pliers.

Remove any protective wax coating from a wooden clothespin with fine sandpaper. Decorate the clothespin with paint or markers. Apply the eye hook and key ring to the top. Close up the hook with pliers.

Buoy Key Ring

Materials: Pill bottle, cork to fit bottle, spray paint, reflective tape, key chain, waterproof glue, drill.

Spray paint a pill bottle. Remove the cap and glue the cork in its place with waterproof glue. Drill a hole through part of the cork that sticks out and insert a key chain. Add reflective tape so that you can find the buoy key ring in the dark.

Fabric Crayon T-Shirt

Materials: T-shirt, Fabric Crayons, plain paper, iron.

Color a picture on plain paper using Fabric Crayons. Remember, the picture will come out in reverse on the T-shirt, so if you use a name or numbers as part of your design, draw them backwards!

Lay the picture wax-side down on a T-shirt, and put a layer of newspaper inside the shirt. Iron for 30 seconds at a hot setting. Your picture will transfer to the T-shirt. Let the pattern set 1-2 days before washing.

Macaroni Name Tags

Materials: ABC macaroni (No. 18), glue, balsawood, art knife, food coloring, pin back closure.

Cut balsawood to the size name tag you want. Use the macaroni as is or color it by dipping it into water dyed with food coloring. Allow the dyed macaroni to dry thoroughly. Allow the dyed macaroni to dry thoroughly. Spell out the names for the tags with the macaroni before glueing them down. Once you have the spacing worked out on the name tag, glue the macaroni to the balsawood. When the glue has dried, glue a pin back closure to the back side of the name tag.

Super Stones

Materials: Smooth stones or rocks, poster paints, brushes, white glue, clear varnish spray.

Gather smooth stones or rocks on a tribal hike or beach outing. Prepare stones for painting by washing and drying them thoroughly. Mix poster paint with white glue, using 2 parts paint to 1 part glue to make an adhesive paint that will stick well to the stones.

You create super stones by first painting a background color on the stones and, after the color has dried, adding a design. Or you can just paint the design on the stone, using the stone's natural color as the background.

Spray the stone with a clear varnish for a glossy finish when the paint has dried. Super stones are good paperweights and decorative table pieces.

Weather Guide

Materials: 5'' x 5'' piece of wood for base, 3 straight branches about 8'' long, small rock, string or thong, glue, drill, scissors, marker, paper (optional).

Drill 3 holes in the base about ½'' deep. Glue branches in the holes and tie them at the top in a tepee fashion. Tie the string or thong to the rock and hang it from the middle of the branches. Write the following instructions on the base or on a piece of paper that you glue to the base.

Place outside on a level surface. If rock is:
  Wet—It's raining.
  White—It's snowing.
  Hot—It's hot outside.
  Cold—It's cold outside.
  Moving—It's windy.
  Hard to see—It's foggy.
  Shaking—There's an earthquake.

GAMES AND TOYS

These projects can be done at tribal meetings. They not only provide an opportunity to teach parents and children new games and skills but also can be used for parent-child interaction at home.

Acorn Toss

Materials: Paper cup, paints and paint brush or crayons, 15'' piece of yarn or string, acorn, drill, large needle.

This game is easy to make and easy to play; however, it takes a little practice. Decorate the paper cup with Indian art designs. Punch a hole at the top edge; tie on the yarn or string (the yarn is springier). Drill a hole through the acorn and thread the other end of the yarn through it using a large needle; then tie a knot. Hold the cup in one hand, and try to flip the nut into it.

Ball Catch

Materials: 1 yard of rubber line, small ball, ice pick, 1' stick, small juice can, screw, leather thong, drill.

Poke a hole through the rubber ball with an ice pick. Push one end of the rubber line through the small ball and knot it. Drill a hole at each end of the stick. Tie the other end of the rubber line to the stick. Fasten the small juice can to the end of the stick with a screw. Tie the leather thong in a loop for a handle at the other end of the stick. Try to flip the ball into the can. You can decorate the various parts of this game if you wish.

Scoop Catch

Materials: 2 round cereal boxes, knife, tempera paints and paint brush, small rubber ball, tape (optional).

Cut part of one side of the boxes away to make a scoop. Paint both boxes with Indian symbols, designs, or other decorations. You may want to tape the rough edges. You and another player can toss a small rubber ball back and forth with the scoops. Start a few feet apart and gradually increase the distance.

Beanbag Toss

Materials: 18'' x 24'' piece of ¼'' plywood or cardboard, several 6'' squares of cloth in different colors, dry beans, needle, thread, paints, paint brush, saw or art knife.

Draw a picture of a bear's (or wolf's) head on the wood or cardboard. Cut 4 holes at least 5'' in diameter for eyes, nose, and mouth. Paint the animal's head on the board and place point numbers of 5 under each eye, 10 under the nose, and 5 under the mouth.

After the paint dries, stand board up against the wall or on a chair. Sew cloth squares together with needle and thread, leaving one side open, and fill the bag with dried beans. Sew remaining side closed. Decorate bags with paints. Toss bags at the board, trying to get them into the holes.

Tic-Tac-Toe

Materials: 2'' x 4'' wood beam, sandpaper, colored golf tees, drill, markers.

Cut square blocks of wood from 2" x 4" beam before the meeting. Sand the edges smooth. Draw 6 boxes in a tic-tac-toe pattern and drill a hole in the center of each box. Use colored golf tees for the markers.

Clothespin Wrestlers

Materials: 2 round wooden clothespins (not the spring type); large, wide rubber bands; markers, paints and paint brush, or crayons.

Have the children decorate clothespins to resemble wrestlers. Loop a rubber band around a pair of the clothespins and twist them in opposite directions. Toss them onto a table and let them spin, jump around, and unwind. The one on top is the winner. Landing side by side is a draw.

Indian Stick Dice

Materials: 3 pieces of wood or cardboard (1½" x 4" x ¼"), paints and paint brush or watercolor markers, varnish (optional).

Indians have played with dice for at least 2,000 years. Indian dice have only two sides: One side is blank and the other side is carved, painted, or decorated with different shapes.

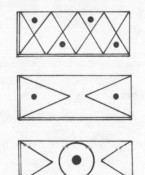

Decorate one side of each piece of wood or cardboard with Indian designs and geometric shapes. Leave the other side blank. If desired, varnish each side.

To play, toss all 3 sticks in the air at once. Score as follows:

    3 designs = 10 points
    2 designs and 1 blank = 2 points
    1 design and 2 blanks = 3 points
    3 blanks = 5 points

Jar Lid Skill Game

Materials: Large, clean jar lid; postcards, greeting cards, or wrapping paper glued to a lightweight cardboard; hole-punch; BBs or small ball bearings; clear plastic wrap; tape; glue; scissors.

Choose an appropriate picture and cut it to fit the inside of the lid. Punch several holes in the picture. Glue it in place. Add the same number of BBs or small ball bearings as there are holes. Cut a circle of plastic wrap a little larger than the lid. Stretch and tape it tightly over the lid. Try to land a ball bearing in each hole by tipping the lid back and forth.

Bottle Cap Snake

Materials: 4' of heavy string, needle, 100 bottle caps, 2 pieces of soft wood 1¼" in diameter, drill, punching tool, carving tool.

Punch a hole in the center of each bottle cap. Using the 1¼" blocks, carve a snake head from one block and a tail from the other. Drill a hole through the snake head lengthwise from the back of the head out through the mouth; drill a hole through the large end of the tail. Tie one end of the string to the tail and thread the string through the bottle caps, tying a knot before and after each one to hold it in place. Pass the thread through the snake head. Tie a knot at the end of the snake's mouth, leaving 1'' of string for the tongue.

Sailboat

Materials: Cork, straight pin, tack, paper, scissors.

Use the pin for the mast, the cork for the hull, and the tack for the ballast on the bottom of the cork. Cut a triangle out of paper and fasten it to the pin for a sail. Children can race their sailboats in a dishpan of water, with all of them blowing to provide the wind.

Boat

Materials: Milk carton, knife, string, paper plate, crayons.

Use a paper milk carton—either the quart or half-gallon size. Rinse it out well. With a knife, cut down one long edge of the milk carton and diagonally across the top and bottom. Hinge

open the carton until it lies flat. The top of the carton will be the front of the boat.

Make another knife cut about ⅓ of the way back from the front of the boat to accommodate the paper plate sail. The slot should go halfway down through the 2 thicknesses of the carton and be angled slightly to match the angle of the paper plate edge.

With crayons, draw a design on the paper plate. Fit the plate into the slot for the sail. Tie a length of string to the front of the boat so you can tow it to shore.

Talking Cans

Materials: 2 juice cans, 15' string coated with resin, buttons, drill.

Remove the lids from one end of each can and drill a hole in the center of the remaining lids. Insert string and fasten securely to a button on the inside of the can. Use 15' of string coated with resin between the cans. Stretch tightly and talk into one can while someone else listens at the other can.

Paper Bag Falseface

Materials: Paper bags, pencils, crayons, glue, colored paper, scissors, drinking straws.

Slip the paper bag over your head and pinch the bag lightly or mark with a pencil where your nose and eyes are. Remove the bag and cut openings for the eyes and nose. Try on the mask again to check all the openings. Color in features or cut out colored paper and glue them on; the more color the better. Drinking straws make stiff, straight hair.

Animal Race

Materials: Stiff cardboard 10"-12" high, 10' string, pencil, scissors, crayons.

Each person makes an animal that he or she can race at the end of the project. The animals don't all have to be the same, but they should all be about the same size.

Take a piece of stiff cardboard, roughly 10" to 12" high. Draw the animal shape on the cardboard; be certain that the rear legs of the animal are extended back farther than the body or tail. Cut out the shape and punch a hole through the cardboard a little below the animal's head—about where the neck would be (see illustration). The hole should be as big around as a pencil. Decorate the animal any way you wish, making sure to color both sides.

Cut a piece of string about 10' long. Tie one end of the string to a chair or table leg about 10" up from the floor. Thread the other end of the string through the hole in the animal. Hold the loose end of the string in your hand, then pull it tight. By slackening the string a bit and then giving it a small jerk, you can make the animal walk. When the animal gets to the other end of the string, jerk the string up slightly and the animal will flip over and be ready to race back. Have fun with your races!

Genius Gel

Materials: Cornstarch, water.

Genius Gel is a substance that is both liquid and solid at the same time. To make Genius Gel, measure 5 parts cornstarch and 4 parts water. Mix this together with your hands. After the cornstarch is totally dissolved in the water, explore all the unusual things that you can do with this mixture. If you pound your fist on the mixture, it's hard. But if you place a relaxed hand on top of it, the hand will sink as if in quicksand! A chunk of Gel can be broken off as with other hard materials. But if some of the mixture is placed on your hand, it begins to drip off—just like liquid! Genius Gel can be poured like water, and, as it's pouring, you can crack off the drips like a solid.

Snow-Snake Derby for Winter Powwow

Materials: Piece of wood 1¾" wide, 1½" high, and 3½' to 4½' long (make sure it is a soft wood); pocketknife; sandpaper; paint; polyurethane varnish; paint brush; 2 round-head upholstery tacks.

3½' to 4½'

1¾"

1½"

end view

During the winter months of heavy snow and cold weather, Indians had several ways to keep themselves amused. One way involved contests with snow snakes. A snow snake is a long, straight piece of wood carved to resemble a snake. The Indians would throw this snow snake down a long trough made of snow and ice. The Indian who threw the snow snake the farthest was the winner. The game inspired great competitions among the tribes and gave the Indians some of the basic skills they needed to survive in the wilderness. It has been reported that some Indians could throw their snow snakes as far as a mile down this iced track.

The track is a long, straight, narrow bank of snow about 2' high, 1' wide, and as long as needed. The top of the bank is flattened and a chain link is dragged over the flat surface of the bank to make a trough or track in the snow. This trough is then iced to make it as slippery as possible.

Before you can play this old Indian game, you must make a snow snake. Carve your piece of wood into a shape similar to the one in the illustration. Round the bottom corners. If the head is *too high* the snake will roll over when tossed. Make sure it is not top-heavy. This is important so the snake can fit into the icy trough.

Use your imagination to make unique heads. Put upholstery tacks in for eyes. Paint your snake with Indian designs and, last of all, varnish the wood.

Regulations for Snow-Snake Derby

- The snow snake must be made of wood.
- Regulation size is 4½' maximum length, 3½' minimum length; 1¾" maximum width; 1½" body height; and unrestricted head height.
- The snow snake must be similar in shape to the one shown in the instructions above. Spears or pointed sticks are not allowed.
- The snow snake must be painted.
- Any kind of wax, ice, or snow may be added to the snow snake.
- There are no restrictions on weight.
- The snow snake must be thrown underhand.
- Competition is divided according to age and sex.
- Runners are not allowed on the snow snake.
- This is a parent-child project—both should be involved in making the snow snake and playing the game.

Backyard Kite

Materials: Trash bags, ½" flat wood moulding, string, kite string, glue, knife.

Each parent-child team will be able to produce this kite during one long activity session. Take 2 pieces of the lightest weight moulding you can buy—1 piece longer than the other. Place them perpendicular to each other in a cross. Lash them together at the crossing and cut a slot at each of the 4 ends.

Pass string through the slots all the way around the kite frame until you have created a kite shape without the fabric. Tie another piece of string to the top of the kite, stretch it to the bottom, and tie it off. Do the same for the crosspiece. Where these 2 strings cross, tie on your kite string.

Spread out a heavy plastic trash bag. Lay the kite frame face down (string up) on the plastic. Fold over the edges, trim, and glue together. Happy flying!

Popsicle Stick Buildings

Materials: 24" piece of aluminum foil, Popsicle sticks (6 for each group), paper clips (10 for each group).

Divide the group into 4 or 5 teams with at least 2 adults per team. The members of each team sit together in a circle. Give each team the same set of materials (foil, sticks, clips). Each team puts the materials given it on the floor in the middle of its circle.

Without touching the materials, they have 3 minutes to discuss as a team how they are going to build something out of these materials. Remind them that they need to develop a good plan, because when the time comes for them to build their object, they aren't going to be able to talk. Urge them to plan carefully and to try to involve everyone on the team.

Then give each team 3 minutes to build the structure with no talking. When the leader calls "time," ask each team to look at the structures of the other teams. Then ask the members of each group to discuss how they felt about their team, teamwork, planning, and execution.

Jigsaw Puzzle

Materials: Picture, scissors, white glue, measuring cup, mixing bowl, spoon, 10" x 12" sheets of waxed paper.

Choose a picture you would like to make into a puzzle. Your choices are broad—road maps, postcards, posters, magazine covers, book jackets. Cut the picture into puzzle-shaped pieces, taking care not to make them too small.

Mix ¼ cup water and 1 cup glue in a bowl. Stir until smooth. Alongside the bowl, put a number of smooth sheets of waxed paper. Dip the puzzle pieces one by one into the glue. Gently hold each piece up and let the excess glue drip off. Then lay the piece down flat on the waxed paper. After about an hour, lay another piece of waxed paper over the top and weigh it down with books. The glue will dry hard and clear overnight.

 ART

These projects are selected to give parents and children opportunities to explore their artistic talents. The finished products can be framed, put in a scrapbook, or displayed at the meeting or at home for all to see. Children and parents should let their imaginations go.

Finger Painting

Materials: Finger paints, finger painting paper, aprons to protect clothes, newspapers or other covers to protect tables and floors.

This is great fun for both parents and children. Allow plenty of time for cleanup, though, because the young artists tend to get fully involved in their work. This is a good project to encourage those children and parents who are shy about their abilities.

Painting

Materials: Paper, watercolors, markers, rags, brushes, glasses or paper cups to hold water.

Youngsters love to draw and paint with watercolors as well as enamels. Be sure to have plenty of paper available and keep rags handy for any emergency spills. Painting pictures of camping trips, family scenes, and animals are all worthwhile efforts that allow parents to help their children while encouraging maximum creative expression.

Sand or Salt Painting

Materials: Pencil, colored sand or salt, glue, colored poster paint, paint brush, heavy cardboard or board.

Pencil in a design on the board, then fill in the design with selected materials. If you use *colored sand*, paint adequate glue on all areas needed for a single color. Pour sand on these areas, allowing them to dry for a few seconds. Then tip the board to eliminate all loose sand. Paint glue on the next areas requiring a different color sand. Repeat procedure until project is completed.

If you use *salt*, generously paint all the areas that will be the same color. Immediately pour salt on the wet surfaces. Let the paint dry for a few seconds, then shake excess salt off the picture. Repeat this process with remaining colors until the project is completed. Salt glistens more than sand.

Note. The poster paint dries very fast. If necessary, paint a small area, pour the salt on it, and continue painting and salting small areas at a time until the project is finished.

Cellophane Stained Glass Window Decorations

Materials: Construction paper, scissors, cellophane (various colors), clear Contact paper, white glue, tagboard patterns to trace (optional).

Place 1 piece of construction paper on top of another, or take 1 piece and fold it in half. Trace a design—animal shape, star, diamond, circle, and so forth—on 1 piece or side of the construction paper. Either cut the design outline within the pieces of paper or cut out two identical design silhouettes and make matching holes in the center.

Cut colored cellophane into small pieces, no larger than 1″ across. Cut a piece of clear Contact paper slightly larger than the hole in your original design. Peel off the back of the Con-

tact paper and place it on the table with the sticky side up. Arrange the cellophane pieces side by side, leaving no space between, until the entire piece of Contact paper is covered. It is helpful to leave a small sticky border around the edge.

Stick the decorated Contact paper between the construction paper outlines to fill the precut hole. Glue the construction paper edge together to frame the cellophane. This will give the craft the look of stained glass. To display, hang the design near a light or in a window.

Wood or Soap Carving

Materials: Well-sharpened knife or carving tools, soap or soft wood, sandpaper.

Instruct the children in the safe use of carving tools before you attempt this project. Draw an outline of a small animal on the soap or soft wood (cedar, basswood, white pine, ash, and sumac are good carving materials). Carve out the animal in as much detail as you wish. Smooth off the rough edges with sandpaper.

Lanterns

Materials: Rectangles of construction paper, scissors, tape, or stapler.

To make the lanterns, fold a rectangle of paper in half lengthwise. Cut slits from the fold to within ½" of the open edges. The slits can be of varying sizes. Open and form into a cylinder. Tape or staple the edges together.

Flowers

Materials: Rectangles of construction paper, scissors, glue, stapler.

To form flowers, fold and cut construction paper as for lanterns. Fold the uncut edges under and paste together. Then form the rectangle into a circle and staple the circle closed. Link several flowers together with paper chains.

Fabric Mural

Materials: Colored felt squares, burlap, glue, needle and thread, pins, pencils, fabric scraps, scissors, 2 dowels, construction paper, cord; colored yarn, yarn needles, glitter (optional).

The fabric mural makes an excellent group project for a tribal meeting. This is a large project, and each parent-child team should be responsible for a section.

Design the entire mural on construction paper first. Use this as a pattern to cut out design elements from felt or fabric scraps.

Pin fabric pieces to the burlap, then either glue or sew them in place. Sew on colorful yarn and use glitter or other materials to add detail. Sew in a casing at the top and bottom to hold the dowels. Attach a cord for hanging.

Paper Straw Chains

Materials: Embroidery thread or yarn, needles, white or colored milk straws, colored construction paper, scissors.

Cut straws into various lengths. Cut out fancy shapes from construction paper (flowers, triangles, wings, etc.). Thread the needles with yarn and string straws and paper shapes in alternating sequences. The chains can be used to decorate for a tribal meeting, a birthday party, or other special occasions.

Paper Straw Art

Materials: Paper straws, colored construction paper, glue, scissors.

Cut out geometric or abstract designs from colored construction paper and glue them down on a piece of larger construction paper. Cut up straws and glue them on top of design or overlap the ends, as shown below.

String and Nail Design

Materials: Hammer; 10''-square wood boards; 1'' nails; string, yarn, or rubber bands; sandpaper.

If the wooden board is rough, sand down the surface and edges first. Next, randomly hammer nails into one side of the board, keeping them at least 1'' apart. The nails should be hammered in far enough to hold firmly, leaving about ½'' of the nail sticking out. Now begin weaving the yarn or string among the nails in any desired pattern or design. Let your imagination go!

Ribbon Butterfly

Materials: 1 yard of #40 cotton ribbon of any pattern, cloth-covered wire, 2 chenille stems, scissors.

Cut the ribbon in two 9'' and two 7'' pieces. Fold each piece in half and cut the parts according to the pattern shown in the following illustration. Unfold the cut pieces.

Place Top #2 on Top #1. Gather the 2 pieces up in the center and wire them together. Attach Bottom #1 and Bottom #2 in the same way. Wire the assembled bottom of the butterfly to the assembled top.

Cut a chenille stem in half. Fold one half into a "V" shape around the center of the butterfly, twist to secure, and shape to form the antennae. Wrap the other chenille stem around a pencil to form a coil, leaving 1" on each end to attach to the butterfly for a body.

Pipe Cleaner Model

Materials: Pipe cleaners of different colors, scissors.

The simple but imaginative use of pipe cleaners to depict animals, birds, fish, and other creatures is a good overnight project.

ADDITIONAL RESOURCES

Resources for craft ideas are limited only by the amount of time you have to do research. You can begin by consulting the books listed here:

Alkems, C.J. (1972). *Crafting with nature's materials.* New York: Sterling Publishers.

Beegle, S. (Ed.). (1966). *Creative craft ideas for all ages.* Cincinnati: Standard Publishing.

D'Amato, J., & D'Amato, A. (1972). *American Indian craft inspirations.* New York: M. Evans.

Hunt, W.B. (1968). *The Golden Book of crafts and hobbies.* New York: Western, Golden Press.

Hunt, W.B. (1973). *The complete how-to book of Indian craft.* New York: Macmillan, Collier Books.

Macfarlan, A.A. (1961). *Living like Indians.* New York: Bonanza Books.

Minor, M., & Minor, N. (1978). *The American Indian craft book.* Lincoln, NE: University of Nebraska Press.

Wiseman, A. (1973). *Making things: The handbook of creative discovery* (Book 1). Boston: Little, Brown.

Wiseman, A. (1975). *Making things: The handbook of creative discovery* (Book 2). Boston: Little, Brown.

See the Appendix for a list of addresses of craft material suppliers.

Games

Games are an important part of all tribal meetings. Children look forward to and enjoy games, and parents often have as much fun as the children. Parents find that playing games with their sons or daughters provides an excellent opportunity to understand their children better.

Games selected for tribal meetings should be well planned, related to the children's skill level, and tested by the host before being introduced at the meeting. Involve your own children as much as possible in the selection of games.

Games provide opportunities for fun as well as teach coordination and teamwork. They foster a friendly and informal atmosphere at meetings. If games are planned after the formal portion of the meeting, they allow children to let off steam and can make the rest of the meeting easier to manage.

CHECKLIST FOR ORGANIZING AND LEADING GAMES

The following guidelines can help you organize and lead games successfully without losing either the children's interest or control of the meeting.

- For best results and the most fun, choose a game in which parents and children participate actively.

- Consider the skill level of all the children in the tribe. Make sure that the game will not put any player in a bad light because he or she cannot physically manage the skills required. Games should help participants feel successful at what they do.
- Understand the game and know the rules.
- Be ready to bend or adapt the rules if necessary.
- Have all the equipment or materials needed on hand ahead of time.
- Mark off boundaries and goals—use masking tape indoors, use flour outdoors.
- Demonstrate the game to the group. Make sure everyone understands the rules of play.
- Don't play the game too long. Stop when the interest and excitement is high—the memory of the fun will last longer.

INDOOR GAMES

These games can be played at meetings, during rainy or winter weather, on camp-outs when there is adequate space inside, or in other indoor locations. They are easy to learn and play and can help you get the meeting started.

Pick-up-Wampum

Materials: Large bowl, kitchen spatula, 25 marble-sized cotton balls; blindfold (optional).

Set the bowl on the floor or on a table and scatter the cotton balls around it. At a given signal, either parent or child takes the spatula and tries to get as many cotton balls into the bowl as possible in 20 seconds. For more fun, blindfold the person trying to get the balls into the bowl.

Scrambled Birch Bark

Materials: 2 identical newspapers.

Divide the tribe into 2 teams and give each a scrambled newspaper. The object is to be the first to reassemble the newspaper in proper order within a given time limit. Teamwork is needed.

Scrambled Moccasins

Materials: 1 shoe from each adult.

Place all the shoes in the center of the room and scramble them up. At a signal, the children rush to find their parents' shoes. The first child to get the shoe back on the parent's foot is the winner.

Alternative: A noncompetitive version of the game is to see how long it takes the children to get all the shoes back to the parents. Repeat to see if the first record can be broken.

Indian Rooster Fight

Materials: Masking tape, ribbons, safety pins.

Mark a 4' circle with masking tape. Pin different colored ribbons to the backs of 2 persons. Turn them to face each other in the circle. They cannot leave the circle. The object is to be the one who finds out the other person's color first.

Ghost Guess

Materials: 1 sheet.

Divide into teams. One side leaves the room, then sends 1 member back into the room under a sheet. The other side tries to guess who it is. Only 1 guess is allowed. If they are right, they get a point. If wrong, the point goes to the other team. Hint: Encourage the players to switch shoes, change height by crouching down, or try to look heavier or thinner.

Crazy Artist

Materials: Paper, crayons or markers.

Provide each team with a crayon or marker. The object is for the whole team to draw a house on a piece of paper. The catch is that each person can only draw 2 straight lines at a time. The house judged the neatest or best is the winner.

Ring Toss

Materials: Clothespins, rubber jar ring.

Each parent holds a clothespin while his or her son or daughter tries to ring the clothespin with a rubber jar ring. Parents may move the pin to try to catch the ring.

Clever Feet Relay

Materials: 2 chairs, 2 pop bottles.

Set chairs about 3' apart. In front of each chair draw 2 circles about 1' apart and 4'' in diameter. Put a soda pop bottle in each circle.

Divide the tribe into 2 teams, 1 for each chair. Have a starting line about 10' to 20' from the chairs. At a signal, the first person from each team runs forward, sits in a chair, and tries to move the bottle from one circle to the other using only his or her feet. Once the bottle has been moved and is upright, the person runs back to his or her team and the next person goes. The first team to finish is the winner.

Paper Cup and Plate Balancing

Materials: Paper plates and cups.

Each parent, taking turns, sits on the floor with feet extended and head back. The parent's child then tries to balance as many plates and cups on the parent's forehead as possible. Start with a plate and then alternate cups and plates. Select someone to keep track of how many cups and plates are balanced before they fall. Once they fall, the parent and child reverse position and balance more plates and cups on the child's head. The team with the most points (1 per plate/cup) is the winner.

Balloon Volleyball

Materials: String, balloon, 2 chairs.

Divide the room lengthwise and tie a string between 2 chairs. Divide the tribe into 2 teams that sit on the floor on opposite sides of the string. A balloon is used as the volleyball, and the string is the net; no spiking is allowed. All players must remain seated at all times.

Newspaper Cutouts

Materials: Newspaper.

Give each parent-child team a sheet of newspaper. Have each team fold and tear out pieces, making a design. Give a prize for the best parent-child design.

Flying Feather

Materials: Downy feather.

Parents kneel so that their heads are no higher than their children's heads when the children are standing. Players face each other and join hands, and the leader throws up a downy feather between them. The parent and child, holding hands at all times, try to keep the feather in the air by blowing.

Alternative: Divide the tribe into 2 teams. Each team forms a circle, holding hands. See which team can keep the feather up the longest.

Tin Can Toss

Materials: Tin can, nail, plywood board, bottle caps.

Nail a tin can onto a board. Have the children toss bottle caps into the can for points. Set the distance from the can with one line for the children and another line that is farther back for the adults. This is a good game to play before the meeting.

Guess Who

Materials: Pictures from magazines, safety pins.

Cut out animals, buildings, cars, and the like from magazines, and pin the pictures on the backs of children and adults. By asking questions of the others, parents and children discover who or what they are.

Potato Bowling

Materials: Newspaper, masking tape, potatoes.

Spread a sheet of newspaper on the floor and mark with masking tape one line 6' away and another 10' away from the paper. Children stand at the 6' line and try to roll a potato so that it stops on the paper. Adults try to roll from the 10' line. Each member has 3 tries.

Eagle Beak's Nose

Materials: Large cloth or sheet with small holes in it.

Hang a large cloth or sheet with a small hole cut in it across a doorway. Each parent puts his or her nose through the hole and the children try to identify which nose belongs to which parent. You can have the parents guess the children's identities as well.

Balloon Battle Royal

Materials: Inflated balloons, string, scissors.

Tie inflated balloons to the waists of the parents and the children. At a beat from the drum, everyone tries to burst everyone else's balloon and protect his or her own. Both bumping and grasping balloons are permissible. The one who keeps his or her balloon the longest wins.

Follow the Sachem

The tribe forms a circle with chairs fairly close together. The tribe then chooses a person to be IT; that person leaves the room. After this person leaves, the group decides upon a person to be the sachem or leader. The leader then begins to make body motions (e.g., slapping hands on knees, moving head up and down, moving feet), and the person who is IT is brought back into the room.

The leader must change motions every 15 seconds or so, and the group must follow. The idea is for the person who is IT to find out who the leader is. The followers should be careful not to give away the leader by looking directly at him or her, but rather should look out of the corners of their eyes or watch someone across from them who is watching the leader. IT has 1 guess for the leader each time the motion is changed.

Do This—Do That

The leader takes a position for directing drill movements with arms, legs, or body, and tells the group to follow him or her whenever a motion is preceded by "Do this" but not to follow the movement when preceded by "Do that." The group holds the former position when a "Do that" command is given. The exercises should be snappy.

Alternative: Substitute the words "Simon says" for "Do this." For example, "Simon says touch your toes." Any command given without "Simon says" should not be followed.

Drum Chairs

Materials: Drum, chairs.

This is a variation on musical chairs. Substitute a drum for the music; otherwise the game is the same. Set up a line of chairs, 1 less than the number of members in the tribe. The tribal members walk around the chairs to the drum beat until the beat stops, then all scramble for a chair. The person who does not get a chair is out, and 1 additional chair is removed from the circle. Changes in tempo and abrupt stops in beat give the game added suspense.

Alternative: Place cards with various instructions for movements, noises, and so forth on all the chairs. Make sure there are as many chairs as there are members. When the drum stops, each person takes a seat and then does whatever his or her card instructs (e.g., push-ups, jumping jacks, duck walk, animal noises, etc.). No one is eliminated from this game.

Almond Race

Materials: 2 bowls of almonds, 2 nut-crackers, 2 chairs.

This is a relay race using a bowl of almonds and a nutcracker. Divide the tribe into 2 teams. Place a bowl of almonds and a nut-cracker on each of the chairs at the other end of the room. At a signal, the first person in each line races to the bowl, shells a nut, eats it, and then returns to tag the next one in line. The first team to get through the line with each member's having shelled and eaten a nut wins.

Magic Noise

A person is chosen to be IT and goes out of the room. The group selects an object and hides it around the room. IT returns to the room and starts to search for the object, getting clues from the buzzing of the tribe. The farther he or she is from the object, the softer the buzz; the nearer, the louder the buzz.

Keen Eyes

Divide the tribe into 2 teams. The teams start out by facing each other in straight lines. Each team studies and tries to memorize how members of the other team are dressed. The teams then go into separate rooms, and the members rearrange their appearance by moving, changing, or swapping articles of clothing. For example, they might exchange vests, untie shoes or put them on the wrong feet, or remove glasses. The teams then get together again. Each person on the team takes a turn pointing out something different about any member of the opposing team. A scorer keeps track of right and wrong observations.

Balloon Relay

Materials: Balloons, 2 chairs.

Blow up enough balloons in advance so there is 1 for each person. Place the chairs at the end of the room. Line up the players in 2 lines for relays. Give each player a blown-up balloon.

At the starting signal, each player in turn runs to the chair and breaks his or her balloon by sitting on it. When the balloon is broken, that player returns to the line and the next player has a turn. The first team to break all of its balloons is the winner.

Ring on a String

Materials: Strong string or twine, ring or washer.

Use a string long enough to make a circle that all members of the tribe can hold on to at the same time. Choose 1 person to stand in the center of a circle formed by the rest of the group. Pass the string around to form a circle on the inside of the group circle.

The person in the middle closes his or her eyes while the ring is placed on the string and passed from person to person. If the string is held tight enough, the ring cannot be seen. The person who is in the middle opens his or her eyes and has 3 guesses to find out where the ring is. If the person finds the ring, he or she trades places with the person who has it. If the person does not find the ring, another player is chosen to stand in the middle of the circle.

Dog and Bone

Materials: Object to be used as bone.

Choose one person to be the "dog." This person is blindfolded and seated on a chair with his or her back to the others. The object of the game is for someone to sneak up to the "dog" and place any object (the "bone") under the chair without being heard by the "dog." If the "dog" hears someone, he or she shouts "bow-wow," and the person who is caught returns to his or her seat. Anyone who places the bone without being caught becomes the "dog."

Balloon Rocket Contest

Materials: Balloons, markers.

Each person chooses a balloon and marks it with his or her initials. All line up on one side of the room with a deflated balloon in hand. Each person then inflates the balloon, holding the open end tightly. On a signal, all balloons are released at once. The person whose balloon travels the farthest is the winner.

Ditto

The tribe sits in a circle. One person starts by making a particular motion such as clapping. The person to the right immediately makes the same motion. The next player continues the motion until everyone around the circle is doing it. Once the motion has gone completely around the circle, the leader changes the motion to start a new one going around the circle.

Ping-Pong Blow

Materials: Table, Ping-Pong ball.

Divide the group into 2 teams, placing 1 team of adults and children on each side of a table. Place a Ping-Pong ball in the center of the table. The object of the game is for each team to blow the ball off the table on its opponent's side. Only blowing is permitted; hands must be kept out of play. Each time the ball

goes over the opponent's side of the table, the other team scores 1 point. Set a total of 5, 7, or 10 points as the winning score.

This Is My Nose

The leader stands in the center of the circle of players. He or she spins around and then stops in front of 1 person, points to some part of his or her own body, and calls it by the name of another part. For example, the leader says, "This is my nose," pointing to a knee.

The person addressed has 10 seconds to point to the part of his or her body named and call it by the name of the part to which the leader pointed. In response to the same example above, the person says, "This is my knee," pointing to the nose. If the person does not do this by the count of 10, he or she becomes the leader.

The Boiler Burst

Everyone in the group except the storyteller sits on a chair in a circle. The storyteller stands in the center of the circle and starts a story. Somewhere in the tale this person says, "The boiler burst," at which point everyone must change seats while the storyteller tries to get a seat. The person left without a chair becomes the next storyteller. He or she can either start a new story or continue where the previous one left off.

7-Up

Materials: 7 erasers or other objects.

Choose 7 or fewer people to be IT. The leader asks everyone else to sit down, close their eyes, and put their heads down. Those who are IT quickly tiptoe around, placing the 7 objects in front of 1 or more persons.

When all objects are placed and the 7 players have returned to the front of the group, the leader calls "7-Up." All those with objects in front of them must stand up. The leader then asks those standing to identify, one at a time, who gave them the object. If they are correct, they change places with the person they identified and become part of the IT group. If they are wrong, they sit down. When all have guessed, those who are IT pick up the objects and the game begins over again.

Pantomime

Materials: Wristwatch or stopwatch, slips of paper, 2 pencils.

Divide the group into 2 teams. Each team selects 4 or 5 popular songs and writes each name on 1 slip of paper. A person on one team draws one of the slips, then has 2 minutes to act out the name of the song for his or her team to guess. The person may not sing it or say any of the words. The team may ask only those questions that can be answered by yes or no by the person acting out the name. The 2 teams take turns acting out the song titles until all of them have been solved. The team that took the least amount of time to guess the song titles wins.

Name Game Bingo

Materials: 1 ruled chart for each player, 1 pencil for each player, slips of paper for the names, bowl or box, colored construction paper squares or unpopped popcorn.

Name Game Bingo is a handy way to introduce people to one another and to speed the learning of each other's names during the first tribal meeting. You can play the game with as few as 9 and as many as 40 members.

Have each person write or print his or her name on a small slip of paper, which is collected and put into a box or bowl. Then give a sheet of paper (8½" x 11") to each participant that has been divided into squares, at least 1 for each of the people attending.

All the players, armed with their charts, go around the room asking for the other players' first names. They write or print these on their charts in any box, obtaining as many different names as there are squares. (Unless the number of players matches the number of squares on the charts exactly, not everyone's name will be on every chart.) Allow adequate time for this name collecting. The whole idea is for group members to get to know one another. When the name collecting is completed, hand out colored construction paper squares to each person. Each square should be the size of 1 square on the chart. (You can use unpopped popcorn instead.)

When the charts and colored squares are ready, the leader draws out one of the slips from the box and calls out the name written on it. The person whose name is called identifies himself or herself. Any player who has that name on his or her chart places 1 of the colored squares (or popcorn kernels) over it. The leader continues to draw until at least 1 player covers all the names in a row, either vertically,

horizontally, or diagonally, as in Bingo. When this happens, the winning player shouts "Name Game!"

To play the game again, players simply clear their charts and the leader puts the name slips back into the box.

Alternative: During the name-collecting period, have the members write down not only the person's name but also 1 particular thing about him or her. This activity helps each person to remember the others and may initiate later conversations.

Scavenger Hunt

Divide the group into 2 teams. Each team forms a circle, and a leader stands between the circles at an equal distance from each. The leader calls for an article such as a comb, belt, penny, white shoe, green shoe, and so forth. The adult or child who finds the article hands it to the player next to him or her, thus passing it around the circle so that all players handle it. When the article returns to the first player, he or she hands it to the leader. The team that gets the article to the leader first scores 1 point. Play to as many points as you wish, or set a goal of 7 points for the winner.

OUTDOOR GAMES

These games are great for outdoor fun, and they teach children and parents teamwork, coordination, and new skills. Use them on camp-outs, at meetings held during warm weather, on weekend trips, or during any other time when the tribe is outdoors.

Treasure Hunt

Materials: Objects to serve as treasure, paper, markers.

Form teams of 3-5 members each and name each team. Write each team's name on a piece of paper, and put the names in a hat. Each team draws 1 name from the hat so that there are pairs of teams. First the teams each decide on a "treasure" and have 15 minutes to hide it. They then create a treasure map to give to their partner team to help them find the treasure. When each team has hidden its treasure and created a map, the leader gives the signal and the great treasure hunt begins. Set a limited time to find the buried treasure.

Steady Head Race

Materials: 1 empty can for each player.

Give each player an empty can. At the start of the race, the players balance the cans on their heads. Without using their hands, players must walk to the finish line with the cans still balanced on their heads. If a can drops off, the player must start over. The race can be an individual, team, or relay event.

Crows and Cranes

Materials: Flour for marking a playing field.

Divide the players into 2 teams: the "Crows" and the "Cranes." Mark a field of play in the following manner:

A = Crows' goal line
A' = Crows' starting line
B = Cranes' goal line
B' = Cranes' starting line

The members of each team line up on their starting line with one foot touching the line. The leader calls either "Crows" or "Cranes." Members of the team called must try to get to their goal line before being caught by pursuing members of the other team. If they are caught, they become members of the opposing team. Play continues until only 1 team remains.

Steal the Moon

Materials: Handkerchief or other article.

Form 2 lines about 15' apart. Both lines should have an equal number of players. Number the members of each line from left to right, and have them face each other. Draw a small circle in the center between the 2 teams, and place a handkerchief or other article in the circle. The leader calls out a number, and the players with that number rush toward the circle.

The object is to grab the handkerchief or article first and make it back to your own line without being tagged by the other player. Two points go to the team if the player gets back without being tagged; 1 point is given to each team if the player gets tagged. The leader can call more than 1 number.

Pass the Grapefruit (or Orange)

Materials: Grapefruit or orange.

Form 2 circles. Choose 1 person to be the leader in each circle. The leader from each team is given a grapefruit or large orange. He or she passes the fruit to an adjacent player without using the hands by placing the fruit under the chin and holding it there by clamping down with the chin. The fruit is passed from player to player around the circle. If the fruit is dropped it goes back to the leader and the game starts again. Alternate parents and children, trying to place parents next to their own sons or daughters.

Nail Driving Relay

Materials: 2 hammers, nails, 2 blocks of wood.

Divide the group into 2 teams, and give each team a block of wood in which an equal number of nails have already been started. Give the first player on each team a hammer. On a signal, the player hits the nail, but is allowed only 1 blow. After 1 hit, he or she passes the hammer to the next player, who also hits the nail with only 1 blow. The team continues to pass the hammer around until all the nails are driven into the board. Only nails driven in straight count, so encourage the players to continue even if the other team drives in all their nails first.

Over-Under Relay

Materials: Object (beanbag, basketball, etc.) to be passed.

Divide the tribe into 2 teams. Alternate the parents and children in each team in a straight column, one behind the other. The first player hands the object over his or her head to the player behind him or her. The second player passes the bag or ball through his or her legs to the third player. The team members continue over-and-under passing until the bag or ball reaches the last player. That player runs to the front of the column and starts the relay all over again. Play continues until all players are back in their original order. The first team to finish wins. You can also play the game by passing overhead only or under only.

Duck, Duck, Goose

The group sits in a circle. Choose 1 person from the group to be IT. He or she runs around the outside of the circle tapping each player on the head and saying "duck" until he or she picks 1 player and says "goose." The one who is called "goose" jumps up and chases IT around the circle. If he or she makes it back to the open space without being tagged, then the other player becomes IT and starts the game again. If IT is tagged, then the other player sits down and IT begins again.

Shadow Tag

One person chases the other players. This is similar to conventional tag, but instead of tagging another player, the person who is IT must step on that person's shadow.

Crawler Tag

Mark a large circle. One person is IT. None of the players can leave the circle. The tagger must crawl on all fours to catch another player. Once tagged, the player also becomes a crawler. Play continues until all are crawlers. Encourage the taggers to use teamwork.

Glue Tag

This is a conventional tag game except that the boundaries of the game are marked and any player who is tagged sticks to the tagger by hanging on to him or her. Eventually all players are stuck to the tagger like glue. Teamwork by the glued players helps trap those who are not yet stuck.

Dodgeball

Materials: 1 soft rubber ball or volleyball.

All players form a circle. Then 4 players move into the center. Those who form the circle have a soft rubber ball or volleyball with which they try to hit (below the waist) the players in the circle. Players who are hit join the circle. The last one remaining in the center is the winner. Repeat the game until all players have had an opportunity to be inside the circle at the beginning. If the ball goes outside the circle, a nearby player recovers it and passes it to another player in the circle.

Sardines

One player hides while the rest of the players come together in an informal group and count to 100. When the counting is done, they set out to hunt. When 1 player finds the hider, the player secretly joins the hider and both hide from the rest of the group. This continues until all players are hidden with the original hider and are packed in like sardines. When the last

hunter discovers the spot, the game starts over and the first finder becomes the hider.

Call Ball

Materials: Volleyball (or similar ball).

All players are in a circle around 1 player in the center who is holding a volleyball. The center player throws the ball high into the air and calls out another player's name. The player whose name was called then must catch the ball before it bounces more than once. If the player does, he or she replaces the caller. If not, the same caller repeats.

Stalking (Blindman's Buff)

A player who is IT is blindfolded and placed in the center of a circle formed by the rest of the tribe. The object is to sneak up and touch the center player without being caught. This can be played while sitting or standing. Anyone caught trying to touch the blindfolded player switches places with him or her.

Bull in the Ring

Players form a circle. One player, the "bull," is in the center. Players hold hands and form a ring around the "bull." The "bull" tries to break through the circle by rushing, lunging, or pulling at it. He or she cannot duck under the circle. If the "bull" escapes, the players chase the "bull." Whoever catches him or her becomes the next "bull."

Alternative: Whoever lets the "bull" escape becomes the next "bull."

I Spy (Hide-and-Seek)

One player, chosen as IT, shuts his or her eyes and counts to 100 at a chosen base, such as a tree. The other players run and hide. After reaching 100, IT shouts, "Here I come, ready or not. All around the base are IT." The player then tries to find the hiders. On spotting one of the other players, he or she shouts, "I see (*person's name*)," and tries to beat the hider back to base. The person who is IT must call out correctly the name of the person hiding or the hider gets home free. The first player caught is IT the next time.

Streets and Alleys

Materials: Whistle.

Choose 2 players, one to be the runner and the other the chaser. All other players, in rows facing the front, stand in parallel lines with arms outstretched so as to touch hands on either side of them. This makes a series of aisles or "streets."

When the leader blows the whistle or calls "Change," players keep their arms outstretched and make a quarter turn to the right. They now make new aisles or "alleys." Neither runner nor chaser may break through a col-

umn nor duck under the players' outstretched arms. Each time the leader blows the whistle, players turn one-quarter to the right, making "streets" or "alleys."

The fun of the game consists in sudden changes that the leader calls. When a runner is caught, select new players to take the place of the chaser and runner.

Alternatives: (a) When a runner tires, he or she may stop in front of a player who will then become the new runner; or (b) in large crowds, several chasers and runners may be used.

Kick the Can

Materials: Tin can.

The can is a base. A player who is IT stands by the can, shuts his or her eyes, and counts to 100. The other players hide. IT shouts, "Here I come, ready or not," and then carefully leaves the can to try to find the hiders. When IT sees a hider, he or she returns to base, puts 1 foot on the can and says "I see (*person's name*)."

At the same time, the player who has been spotted runs to the base and tries to kick the can before the player who is IT can touch it and call out the player's name. If unsuccessful, the player is put into "jail." If successful, the player is allowed to free any other players from "jail." The goal is to get all the players in "jail." Suggested time limit for the game: 15 minutes.

Stories

The stories in this section can be used to entertain children in a variety of settings—meetings, camp-outs, outings, or car trips. These stories, however, can be more than entertainment; they can provide learning experiences about Indian culture, values, and beliefs. They often can convey a lesson or provoke questions more effectively than more direct methods.

Stories are beneficial to tribes in several ways. They create a common focus for the group, giving members a feeling of togetherness. They also raise questions for group discussion or later parent-child talks, especially about values important to child development and the family. In addition, stories give children a chance to exercise their imaginations.

Storytime easily fits into tribal meetings. One natural place for a story is directly after the opening ritual, when the group is already gathered together and focused. A story can also be an opening for an agenda item that needs discussion. Later in the meeting, it can serve as a way to draw the group back together after a break. As an ending, it can bring up questions for discussion by parents and children following the meeting.

Try to actively involve listeners in the story as you tell it. This reinforces the ideas of the story, exercises the listeners' creativity, and makes the listeners feel a part of the group. Use the following methods to get listeners involved:

- Have them make sounds that coordinate with the story.
- Ask them to pantomime as you tell the story.
- Ask them to finish the story.
- Tell an add-a-line story in which each person in the group adds a line to the ongoing story.

TIPS FOR THE STORYTELLER

Good storytellers are made, not born. The guidelines listed below can help you select and tell stories that fit your audience and keep their attention throughout the session. Look the guidelines over carefully, then practice telling your story to others before the tribal meeting. In time, you will be able to bring these tales to life for your listeners and involve them in the experience.

1. The first step in telling a good story is to find the proper story. Know your audience—their age, sex, and interests—and use this knowledge as a guide for choosing story subjects. Avoid morbid, preachy, or overly sentimental tales. Your story can be taken from history, literature, Indian legends and tales, or even a contemporary news item.

2. After finding the proper story, memorize it so that you can tell it without reading from a book. It's difficult to establish close personal contact with your audience when reading aloud to them. Become familiar with the story until you can visualize each character and each scene in relation to the climax.

3. Tell the tale as dramatically as possible. Use your head, hands, and body to make the story come alive. Change your voice to fit the character or mood; children do not enjoy listening to a monotone narrator. Be sensitive to your listeners' reactions. If they become restless or lose interest, change your voice, speed up the action, ask them if they know what the

characters will do next—use any method to liven up the story and recapture the listeners' interest.

4. Open with a dramatic beginning. It's better to say, " 'Twas a dark and stormy night; four of us huddled around the campfire . . ." than, "I'm going to tell you a story about . . ." Avoid lengthy, long-winded introductions. Get to the point quickly.

5. After the story is finished, ask a few simple questions to make sure the listeners understood the moral or point of your story. Remember, not all stories must have a moral.

6. Arrange the seating so that you are as close to your audience as possible. The children should sit together—elbow to elbow is the rule. Try to ensure you won't be interrupted by any outside noise or confusion; close the door, take the phone off the hook, do whatever you need to do to guarantee private, quiet time with the children.

   If something does interrupt your narrative, treat the incident lightly and proceed with the story. To make sure you have the children's full attention, ask them what was happening in the story when the interruption occurred.

7. End your story with a punch line. Leave the climax for the last paragraph, sentence, or word.

8. Never try to tell a story when the children don't want to hear one. Make storytime one of the treats of the meeting.

9. Never tell a story you don't enjoy telling!

 # Stories

The following stories depict various Indian settings and legends. Many are short and can be told in a few minutes. Try out some of the stories on family members or others before telling them to the tribe. Sample discussion questions follow the first story.

Little Flying Cloud

(From Big Brave's Notebook. *Los Angeles: YMCA of Metropolitan Los Angeles, 1978.)*

Little Flying Cloud didn't lead a very happy life. He couldn't run fast, he couldn't shoot well with bow and arrow, and he was a poor hunter. This was because his father had been killed while hunting buffalo many moons ago and couldn't teach him these things.

Other little braves made fun of him. They teased him and never invited him to play games or hunt in the forest with them. But they soon became curious because many times Little Flying Cloud would slip out of the village and be gone most of the morning or afternoon.

One day they followed him to his hidden cave. From a hiding place, they watched him play with several chipmunks and rabbits that he had tamed. After a time, the other braves came out of hiding and asked Little Flying Cloud to teach them how to tame the wild animals and make them friends. This he did willingly. In no time he became popular with the other little braves because they discovered he knew much more about the small animals of the forest than they did.

The little braves, in turn, gave him special lessons in swimming, shooting bow and arrow, and other skills they had learned from their fathers. Now Little Flying Cloud was happy, and soon he was the best-liked young brave in the entire village.

Sample Discussion Questions

• Can you think of several children in class at school who don't have much fun? Why don't they, do you think? Can you help them? In what ways?

• Is there some boy or girl who lives near you who doesn't have one of his or her parents? Could your mother or father bring him or her along as a "second son/daughter"? If so, how could you help this boy or girl have fun and feel at home in the tribe?

• If your Y-Indian Guide tribe isn't up to full size—nine parent-child teams—do you know someone who might enjoy being invited? How can they be brought to the next meeting? Who will visit them to invite them?

A Friend in Need

"Tell us a story! Please, Wise Father, tell us another of your legends!"

Eagerly the children sat at the feet of Grey Fox, the Chief, to listen and to learn. The Chief smiled at the memory of the story he had chosen to tell and then began:

"Many moons ago two hunters were traveling the trail together. Suddenly they came face to face with a huge bear. One hunter, in great fear and without thought for his companion, climbed a tree as fast as he could and hid himself in the branches.

"The other hunter, seeing that single-handed he was no match for the bear, threw himself on the ground and pretended to be dead. He had heard from other hunters that a bear will not molest a dead body.

"The gruff old bear lumbered toward him, his huge paws slapping the ground with spine-chilling thumps. Soon the shaggy beast stood directly over the man, sniffing at the Indian's nose and ears. With great control, the man held his breath and lay still.

"Soon the bear turned and walked slowly away. As the ponderous animal disappeared from sight, the first hunter came down from his hiding place in the tree and asked his companion what it was the bear had said to him. 'For,' he said, 'I saw that the bear put his mouth very close to your ear and whispered something to you.'

'Why,' replied the other, 'it's no secret. He advised me not to keep company with those who leave their friends and run away when danger is near.'

Grey Fox's eyes twinkled with humor as he ended his story. "What lesson do you find in this tale of the hunting trail?" he asked.

Dead or Alive

(From Twenty Tepee Tales *by M. Lotz and D. Monahan. New York: Association Press, 1950.)*

Many years ago there was an Indian medicine man famous for his wisdom. For many years he had helped the members of his tribe by answering their questions and giving them wise advice. However, because he was so old, many of the young braves of the tribe felt that he ought to give up his position as medicine man and allow a younger brave to have the honor.

Several times the young braves of the tribe had attempted to remove him by asking him questions and posing problems that they hoped he would not be able to answer. If only they could cause him to make a mistake or catch him with a question he would not be able to answer, they were sure they could replace him with a younger man. Each time they attempted to do this, however, they failed. His answers were always right and his advice always trustworthy.

One day, while a group of younger braves was on the hunt, one of the young men turned to the group and said, "Tonight I will ask the old medicine man a question that he will not be able to answer. Gather all our tribesmen before his tepee tonight, and you will see."

The other braves remembered their past failures and wanted to know what he planned to do. The younger brave replied, "I will catch a bird and take it to him, holding it in my hands so that the feathers show through my fingers. I will say to him, 'What have I in my hands?' Seeing the feathers, he will reply, 'A bird.' Then I will say, 'That is correct, but tell me, Wise One, is it dead or alive?' If he says it is dead, I will open my hands and let it fly away. If he says it is alive, I will smother it and drop it, dead, at his feet. So you see, regardless of his answer, he will be wrong, and we will be able to replace him with a younger man."

This pleased the braves; they were certain the plan could not fail. When they returned from the hunt, they spread word around the tribe of the test that the medicine man would face. At sundown the space before the ancient Indian's tepee was crowded with Indians eager for the test.

The young man whose plan it was elbowed his way through the crowd, and, with hands cupped before him, challenged the medicine man to come forth and be tried. The wise man came from his tepee and stood before the throng. "What is it, my son?" he asked.

The young man answered, "It is said that you can answer all questions correctly. If this be so, Father, tell what I have in my hands."

The old man looked and replied, "A bird, my son."

"That is correct," the young brave responded. "But tell me, Father, is it dead or is it alive?"

This was the challenge! All the Indians present held their breath, waiting for the medicine man's answer. The old man paused; then, looking deep into the young man's eyes, he responded, "That, my son, depends on you."

Where the Girl Saved Her Brother

(From The Sound of Flutes and Other Indian Legends, edited by Richard Erdoes. New York: Pantheon Books, 1976, pp. 10-15.)

In the summer of 1876, two of the greatest battles between soldiers and Indians were fought on the plains of Montana. The first fight was called the Battle of the Rosebud. The second battle, fought a week later, was called the Battle of the Little Big Horn, where General Custer was defeated. The Cheyennes call the Battle of the Rosebud the fight *Where the Girl Saved Her Brother*. I'll tell you why.

But first let me explain what is meant when an Indian says, "I have counted coup." Counting coup means riding up to an enemy and instead of killing him, touching him with a feathered stick or your hand. This is a test of great courage and can earn you considerable honor in the eyes of the tribe. One of the greatest acts of counting coup is to dash into the midst of your enemies to rescue a friend,

take him up on back of your horse, and gallop out again, saving his life by risking your own. That is counting big coup, indeed!

At the time of these battles, the whites wanted all Indians to live on reservations. Some tribes, however, decided to fight to stay free. White soldiers were sent to force these Indians to surrender and live on reservation land. Many proud tribes and braves joined together to battle the soldiers.

Among them was a brave young woman, Buffalo Calf Road Woman, who rode proudly at the side of her husband, Black Coyote, when the Battle of the Rosebud began. Her brother, Chief Comes-in-Sight, was in the battle, too. When Buffalo Calf Road Woman looked for her brother in the fight, she saw that his horse had been killed under him and that he was surrounded by white soldiers and their Crow scouts. Although hard pressed on every side, he fought off his enemies with bravery and skill.

Buffalo Calf Road Woman uttered a shrill war cry and raced her pony right through the enemies surrounding her brother. Chief Comes-in-Sight saw her coming and jumped up onto her horse behind his sister. Buffalo Calf Road Woman laughed with joy and the excitement of the rescue. The soldiers fired at them and the Crow scouts shot their arrows— but her horse moved too fast for her or Chief Comes-in-Sight to be hit.

Then she turned her horse and raced up the hill from which the old chiefs and medicine men watched the battle. The Sioux and Cheyenne saw what she had done and the white soldiers saw it, too. They all stopped fighting and watched the brave girl saving her brother's life. The warriors raised their arms and set up a mighty shout—a long, trilling war cry that made one's hairs stand on end. Even some of the soldiers threw their caps in the air and shouted "Hurrah!" in honor of Buffalo Calf Road Woman.

The white General Crook thought, "If their women fight like this, what will their warriors be like? Even if I win, I will lose half my men." And so General Crook retreated a hundred miles or so away from the battleground. When Custer needed him a week later, Crook was far away.

Many who saw what Buffalo Calf Road Woman had done thought that she had counted the biggest coup of all—not taking life but saving it. That is why the Indians call the Battle of the Rosebud *Where the Girl Saved Her Brother*. The memory of her deed lives on—and will live on as long as there are storytellers to tell the tale.

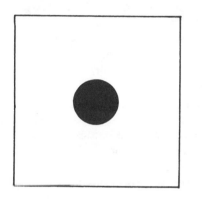

Looking for the Good

(From Program Resource Book. *St. Paul/ Minneapolis: YMCAs of St. Paul & Minneapolis.)*

Chief Silver Maple called together the members of his tribe. They seated themselves in a circle. In the center of the circle, the medicine man was making an Indian sand painting. Most Indian sand paintings are very colorful. They are made during the day and every trace of them must be destroyed before the sun sets. This time, the picture was different. The braves watched in surprise as the medicine man made a square out of white sand and, in the center of the square, poured a large circle of black sand.

The braves whispered to each other, "I wonder what this is."

The Chief heard them talking and called for silence. He asked, "Braves, what do you see here?"

The first brave said, "I see a black spot." The second brave replied, "That is what I see, too." So said each brave around the circle, each agreeing on what the medicine man had painted.

After they had all spoken, the Chief said, "Braves, why is it that none of you noticed this is a white square with a black spot on it? Many of us, as we think about other tribes and as we think about our fellow braves, look for the black spots and fail to see the rest of the picture—the white square. Too often we look for what is bad and do not see what is good. Let us look for the good things in our fellow tribes and in one another from now on."

Stretching the Truth

(From Program Resource Book. *St. Paul/ Minneapolis: YMCAs of St. Paul & Minneapolis.)*

One night Little Otter rushed into the tepee and said excitedly, "Mother, I just saw a thousand deer in the meadow!"

Mother said, "Are you sure? Did you count them?"

"It was so dark, I couldn't count them. I think there were a hundred."

Mother said, "Are you sure, my son?"

"Well, I know there were at least ten," said the little brave.

Then his mother patiently said, "Little Otter, you did not count the deer, how do you know?"

Little Otter became impatient and said, "Well, I know there were two deer anyway, a big buck and a small one."

The Chief of the tribe had listened to the conversation. He now said, "Little Otter, let me tell you a story. When I was a young brave, I was in the habit of stretching the truth because I had not learned the importance of being accurate. In my tribe, the Okeewa, I was responsible for keeping track of the food. As animal meats, herbs, roots, berries, and other foods were brought to me, I would store them in the ground and cover them well.

"One day old Chief Kiyi came to me and asked if there was plenty of food for a big tribal feast and ceremony. In haste I took a quick glance at the food that was stored away in the ground. I did not take time to count the number of carcasses of deer or any of the other food supplies. Instead, I became careless and took a chance in reporting what I saw at a quick glance. I reported to the Chief that there was plenty of food.

"When the day of the big feast came, I was very much embarrassed to find there was a shortage of food, and that many of the mothers, little braves, babies, and even warriors would not have enough to eat.

"The Chief was very angry, as were many of the braves. Had it not been for the quick thinking of Watosa, we would all have been disappointed. Watosa got on his pinto horse and galloped away in a cloud of dust. Soon he returned with his arms loaded with food as well as large bags of food thrown over the back of his horse. He had borrowed much food from a nearby tribe, promising to pay back what he had borrowed.

"To teach me a lesson, the Chief required me to hunt for many days for deer as well as other foods to pay back the borrowed food from the other tribe. From that time on I made up my mind to be more accurate and never to exaggerate."

The Indian and the Cricket

(From Twenty Tepee Tales, *by M. Lotz and D. Monahan. New York: Association Press, 1950.)*

One day an Indian left his home to visit a white man with whom he had become friends. Being in a city, with its noises and its crowds, was a new experience for the Indian, and he was fascinated by it.

The Indian and the white man were walking down the street when suddenly the red man touched his friend's shoulder and said quietly, "Stop! Do you hear what I hear?"

His white friend paused, listened, smiled, and said, "All I hear is the tooting of car horns, the noise of the buses, and the voices of people. Just the regular sounds of the city. What is it you hear?"

The Indian replied, "I hear a cricket chirping somewhere nearby."

Again the white man listened, but shook his head. "You must be mistaken," he said, "I hear no cricket. And even if there were a cricket nearby, the chirping would be drowned out by all these other noises."

The Indian would not be persuaded. After a moment he motioned to his friend, and walking a few steps along the sidewalk, they came to a vine growing on the outside of one of the buildings. He pushed the leaves aside, and

there, to the amazement of the white man, a tiny cricket was revealed, chirping its loudest. Now that he saw the cricket and was close to it, the white man could hear its call.

As they proceeded on their way, he said to his Indian friend, "Of course, you heard the cricket because your hearing is much better than mine. All Indians can hear better than white people."

The Indian smiled, shook his head, and replied, "No, that is not true. The Indians' hearing is no better than that of the whites. Watch! I'll prove it to you."

He reached into his pocket and found a fifty-cent piece, which he tossed to the sidewalk. As it clinked against the cement, people from several yards around them stopped, turned, and looked. Finally, one of them picked up the piece, pocketed it, and went on his way.

"You see," said the Indian, "the noise made by the fifty-cent piece was no louder than that made by the cricket, yet many white people heard the noise the money made, stopped, and paid attention to it, although they paid no heed to the noise made by the cricket. The reason is not a difference in our hearing. It is a difference in what we have learned to listen for, a difference in the things we turn our attention toward."

Trader Jim

(From Program Resource Book. *St. Paul/ Minneapolis: YMCAs of St. Paul & Minneapolis.)*

Did you ever hear of Trader Jim? Trader Jim lived in Boston in the early days. Business was slow in the city. But Jim had heard about the big demand for American furs in Europe, so he decided to close his store and move into Indian country and trade for furs.

After several months of traveling alone, he located an ideal spot of ground in Ohio for a trading post. He built his log cabin on a hill where two big rivers met. After many days and nights of hard work, he completed his store. He stacked his shelves with hardware, salt, sugar, and seeds. Then he waited.

During all this time he had not seen a single Indian. Then, finally, late one afternoon he saw a fleet of canoes coming around the bend of the river. The Indians beached their canoes far below him, and ignored his presence. Dusk fell and the Indians made camp, built fires, and danced. Trader Jim waited . . . and waited. Then he fell asleep.

As the sun rose through the early morning mist, there was a loud rap on the door. A big Indian chief stood alone in the doorway with his arms full of furs. In sign language he counted them to be nine furs. Trader Jim also counted—and recounted—and indicated that there were ten furs with his ten fingers. The chief, however, insisted there were only nine furs and proceeded to select his purchases on this basis. Trader Jim traded for the nine furs and then thrust a large sack of flour into the Chief's arms for the tenth fur and pushed the Chief out the door before he could protest.

It was but a short time later that all the Indians in the camp came to Jim's Trading Post—their arms laden with furs. On his morning trip, the old chief had tested Jim, and Jim's reputation had been established for years to come.

The Unknown Woman

(From Southern Indian Myths and Legends, *edited by Virginia Pounds Brown and Laurella Owens. Birmingham, AL: Beechwood Books, 1985, pp. 54-55.)*

Two Choctaw hunters camped for the night on a bend in the Alabama River. They were tired and discouraged, having hunted for two days and killed only one black hawk. They had no game to take back to their village.

While they were roasting the hawk on a campfire for their supper, they heard a low, plaintive sound like the call of a dove. The sad notes broke the deep night silence again and again. As the full moon rose across the river, the strange sound became more distinct.

The men looked up and down the river but saw only the sandy shore in the moonlight. Then they looked in the opposite direction and to their astonishment saw a beautiful woman dressed in white, standing on a mound. She beckoned to the hunters.

"I'm very hungry," the woman said.

One of the hunters ran to the campfire and brought the roasted hawk to the woman. After she had eaten some, she gave the rest back to them. "You have saved me from death. I will not forget your kindness. One full moon from now, in midsummer, return to the mound where I am standing."

Suddenly a gentle breeze came up, and the woman disappeared as mysteriously as she had come.

The hunters knew they had seen Unknown Woman, the daughter of the Great Spirit. They returned to their village, but kept secret the strange meeting with the woman.

One month later, when the moon was full, the hunters came back to the place where Unknown Woman had spoken to them. As the moon rose over the opposite bank, they stood at the foot of the mound, waiting. But Unknown Woman was nowhere to be seen.

"She has not come as she promised," they said to each other.

Then one hunter remembered. "She told us to come to the very spot where she stood." So the men climbed the mound. They could not believe what they saw; the mound was covered with a plant they had never seen before. It was a tall plant with leaves like knives and delicate tassels emerging from the spike-like fruit or ears. Inside the ears was a delicious food.

So it was that the Choctaws received the gift of corn. They cultivated corn ever afterward and never again were hungry.

Twigs

(From The Tales of Running Deer *by D. Monahan. New York: Association Press, 1970.)*

"What lesson do you have for us tonight, Running Deer?" Little Bear and Red Fox asked the question at the same moment. Other Indian children gathered around Running Deer's fire waiting for the answer. They came to listen and to learn, as was the custom.

"I would speak this night," responded Running Deer, "of a matter that affects us all—the importance of good habits. We all have habits. We must be sure, then, that our habits are good friends that help us live better lives and not enemies that bring unhappiness and problems."

"What are some good habits, Running Deer?" asked Red Fox.

Running Deer looked into the young faces before him and replied, "It is better for you to answer this question than for me to give the answer. Tell me, what habits do you think are your good companions on the trail of life?"

"Honesty is one, I think," answered a young brave sitting across the campfire circle. Soon a chorus of voices offered other answers.

"We have made for ourselves this night a good list of habits that can be counted on as friends to help us live good lives. You have done very well," Running Deer spoke with appreciation.

"Running Deer, the twigs you have beside you there—what are they for?" asked the ever-curious Red Fox.

"They are part of tonight's lesson. Watch and listen. I hope you will allow them to teach you more about habits—good and bad." Running Deer picked up the first of the twigs. "Each of these twigs we shall give the name of a bad habit. What shall this first one be called?"

"Anger," suggested a young voice.

"Anger it is, then," Running Deer announced. With this he easily snapped the twig in two. "You see how single habits can be broken with only a small effort?" he asked.

Picking up two twigs, and with more effort, he broke them. "You see, two combined are harder to break. Watch closely now," he continued. This time he picked up three twigs. Breaking the three together proved even more difficult. Running Deer added another twig and broke four twigs together. Each time he kept adding another twig until he came to a number that he could not break despite his hardest efforts.

"You see," Running Deer said, "I have now combined so many twigs that I can no longer break them. This is true of habits also. A combination of several bad habits—for instance, anger, dishonesty, impatience, laziness, untruthfulness—can become too strong to break all at once. Be sure that your habits are good ones that need no breaking."

"Running Deer," the voice was that of Little Bear. "By breaking one at a time, the entire bundle can be broken, can it not?"

"True, my friend," answered Running Deer. "This is another lesson we can learn from our twigs. If you have bad habits to break, work on them one at a time until all are conquered.

It is also true that good habits can best be achieved one by one."

Wet Feathers

(From Twenty Tepee Tales *by M. Lotz and D. Monahan. New York: Association Press, 1950.)*

Dark clouds rolled out of the west as little Tomahawk walked through the forest near his home. Flashes of yellow lightning danced in the sky, and faraway thunder grew louder. The air was heavy with moisture.

"The clouds will soon be overhead," thought Tomahawk. "I'd better run for the village or I'll get soaked."

He hurried up the path that led to the village. He thought that he would beat the rain, for the wind that comes before a storm was not yet blowing.

A sudden sound made Tomahawk stop. He listened, but all was silent except for the distant roll of thunder. Then, again, he heard the noise; it sounded like a bird in trouble. Searching, he discovered a mallard duck huddled under a bush. The duck did not try to escape from him as he came closer. Looking down, he saw that it had a broken leg. Carefully, he lifted the duck with both hands. In its big brown eyes was a look of fear and pain that would make even a strong man feel sorry for it. Tomahawk quickly tucked the bird under his deerskin jacket and ran for the village. The rain was coming. He would have made the journey faster without the duck, but he remembered how it had looked at him. He held on and ran hard.

Nearly a moon had passed, and the broken leg was completely well. The duck was tame and would run gaily around the wigwam, playing with the Indian children who came each day to see Tomahawk.

The bird had been given a name—"Wet Feathers"—for even though Tomahawk had tried to protect the duck on that rainy day, it had gotten very wet. Tomahawk's father had laughed when he saw the bird and had suggested the name. Actually, he thought it was foolish to have a duck for a pet when it would make such a fine dinner.

Wet Feathers seemed to enjoy its new home, but Tomahawk noticed a longing look in its eye whenever wild ducks, passing overhead, called to it with a loud "honk." So he was not completely surprised when Wet Feathers flew away one day to join its comrades in flight.

Two summers passed. Tomahawk was twelve years old. He had learned to shoot his arrows well and could paddle a canoe with enough skill to please the braves of the tribe.

Each spring the Kickapoo tribe held a canoe race for boys who had not yet reached their eleventh year. Tomahawk stood on the riverbank and watched the race. The young boys of the tribe were straining every muscle, for the winner was to sit at an honored place at the next powwow.

The race was a close one. The river was filled with canoes, and so it was no wonder that many boys were crowded out. Very few people noticed one little fellow who had dropped out right at the start of the race. Not only that, but his paddle was broken.

Later in the day, Tomahawk found this same little boy sitting alone under a big tree, his head in his hands.

"What makes you so unhappy?" asked Tomahawk.

"My father did not expect me to win the race," came the reply, "but he did want me to put up a good fight."

"But you cannot win a race without a paddle," replied Tomahawk.

"I know," said the boy, "but all my father will know is that I did not finish the race. He was not on the riverbank this afternoon."

"But if he wanted you to do well in the race, why did he not come to watch?"

The boy looked up. His eyes were filled with sadness. "Several moons ago, my father was hurt in a fight with a bear. You see, he is blind."

Tomahawk lowered his head. "I am sorry," he said. "I am sorry, too, that you did not do well in the race."

The boy's eyes lighted up. "Perhaps you would come with me and explain to my father about the race. He would understand then how it happened that I did not finish," he pleaded.

"I would be glad to," replied Tomahawk, "but I promised to go fishing with my friend, Clear Sky, this afternoon. I will help you some other time."

As Tomahawk turned to go, he stopped dead still. There in his path stood No-ha-wiss, the great chief of the Kickapoo tribe. The Chief was looking straight at Tomahawk.

"You are Tomahawk," said the Chief. "I remember the time that you found a duck near the river. You cared for it because it was in trouble. Now you find a fellow brave in trouble, but you refuse to help him? Do you care more for a duck than a fellow brave?"

Tomahawk turned and looked at the boy under the tree. The Chief was right. It was his duty to help. A moment later the boys were walking toward the village. They were going to talk to the boy's father.

Why the Frog Has No Teeth and the Woodchuck Sleeps All Winter

(From Program Resource Book. *St. Paul/ Minneapolis: YMCAs of St. Paul & Minneapolis.)*

Once the chief of the squirrel tribe was going through the woods on his regular tour of inspection. When he did this he made himself invisible so that he could find out what was going on. At the foot of a tall pine tree he saw a squirrel, a frog, and a woodchuck engaged in a discussion.

The squirrel was complaining. "Who could have stolen my nuts?" he was saying. "All summer long I have been collecting them; now they are all gone. My nest is empty, swept out clean!"

"What a pity, what a pity!" said the frog, tears rolling down his cheeks.

And the woodchuck made a great bluster and said the culprit ought to be caught.

The chief of the squirrel tribe said to himself, "I'll come around tonight at midnight to investigate further."

That night he came, invisible, and saw the woodchuck digging in his burrow at the foot of the pine tree. After a while the woodchuck stopped and went away; in a few minutes he was back, his cheeks all puffed out. When he came to the hole, he opened his mouth and dropped in the nuts that he was carrying in his cheeks, one by one.

"Where did he get them?" the squirrel chief wondered. "It's a long way from here to a hickory nut tree."

He decided that he would come back at noon

the next day to see what else he could discover.

At noon the next day he was back. There was a little spring near the foot of the same pine tree, and from the pool he saw the big green frog come hopping and disappear behind the tree. In a few minutes the frog came back, his cheeks all puffed out. The squirrel chief saw him move aside a tuft of green moss, drop the nuts that he carried in his cheeks into the hole, and then go back for more.

"So that's what happened to poor squirrel's winter store," said the chief of the squirrels, and he sent out a call for all the animals of the forest to come to a great council to decide what punishment the thieves should receive.

When all the animals were seated around in a great circle, they saw that two were missing—the frog and the woodchuck.

"I'll go and get them," said the chief of the squirrels, and, sure enough, in a few minutes he had brought them to the meeting. The frog was all glistening wet; tears were rolling down from his great round eyes. The woodchuck was in a terrible humor with his whiskers bristling.

Now these two were accused of having stolen the squirrel's winter store, and they had no defense. But what should their punishment be? It was the law of the forest that thievery should be punished with death. Some of the animals, however, thought it would be better in this case to have some punishment that would serve as a reminder to future generations.

So they said to the frog, "You, since you have stolen squirrel's nuts, shall never enjoy eating nuts again." Frog, when he heard these words, hopped off in shame and dejection, while from his mouth the teeth dropped out as he went. Frogs have never had teeth from that day to this.

And they said to the woodchuck, "For you who have stolen squirrel's stores, we have another punishment. You shall sleep all through the winter months, and in the summer you shall eat only grasses and vegetables and fruits."

And that's the way it still is.

Indians Discover Fire

After a little brave had attained a certain age, and before he could become a recognized member of the tribe, he had to show that he was worthy of the honor. He had to go out from the tribe, shift for himself, and, on his return, make a contribution that would be a credit to the tribe.

Early one morning a young brave left the Sioux Nation and traveled many miles before nightfall. He had eaten berries and drunk plenty of water from the cool, clear streams. For several days food was plentiful, but as time passed it became more and more scarce. Yet the young brave had found nothing that would prove a benefit to his tribe. He became discouraged and his hunger increased. Finally, finding a cave, he crawled in, hoping the end would be swift, as he could not return to his people a failure.

He lay on the floor of the cave and dozed a minute. Suddenly he opened his eyes in amazement and jumped to his feet as a huge bear stood before him. It said, "Do not be afraid. I am here to tell you that you will make a great discovery this day. You will go back to your tribe and be named 'Great Bear' in my honor." Suddenly the bear disappeared and a strong wind began to blow. The young brave was drawn to the entrance of the cave, where he saw two trees whipped back and forth by strong gusts of wind. The tempo increased as the winds blew furiously, and soon smoke appeared where the trees were rubbing together. In a few moments the dry grass surrounding the trees burst into flame, blazed brightly, and died as the grass burned out.

The young brave waited no more, but hurried back to his tribe and immediately told the Chief of his experience. The Chief was skeptical, but gave the brave a chance to prove himself. After much rubbing of two sticks and moments of great anxiety, a flame was again produced, and Great Bear became a full-fledged member of the Sioux Nation, holding a place of honor beside the Chief at tribal council meetings.

King of the Forest

Long before the forests knew the footsteps of any human, the squirrel was king of all the woods. Among the beasts he was ruler. He was a magnificent animal. Larger than the largest lion, stronger than the strongest buffalo, swifter than the swiftest deer, wiser than the wisest owl. Indeed, he was truly a ruler. Because of his position, he was admired by all the beasts of the forest.

For many years the squirrel ruled well, but the time came when he became so impressed with his authority that he thought of no one but himself. He no longer ruled unselfishly, but grew in selfishness and cruelty. As time passed, his vanity and cruelty became unbearable. Animals who had once loved him now hated and feared him. The fear and hatred for the squirrel grew until the animals felt it necessary to call a meeting of all the beasts of the forest. At this meeting, a prayer was made to the Great Spirit for help.

Hearing the prayer of these worried beasts, the Great Spirit came to earth in the guise of an animal and called upon the squirrel. He found the squirrel mean and ugly, and so, exercising his magic power, he assumed godly form and stood before the squirrel, who cowered at this display of power. The Great Spirit told the huge king he was no longer worthy to rule over the beasts of the forest and that because of his selfishness and cruelty he must be punished.

With this warning, the Great Spirit cast a spell over the squirrel and the once-towering king became so small that the Great Spirit could hold him in one hand. Picking up the now-terrified animal, the Great Spirit threw him high into a tree, saying, "Henceforth you shall spend your days in the trees. Small in stature, you shall fear every living thing. Your food shall be the nuts and herbs of the forest. No longer will you have your kingly roar, but shall chatter in a harmless voice. A new king will be named—one who shall be kind and wise and humble; who will remain unselfish and gentle despite his authority and strength."

With this, the Great Spirit vanished, leaving behind the small, shy animal we know today as the squirrel.

Coyote and the Fox

One day Coyote was going out hunting, so he picked up his bow and quiver. In his quiver he put five arrows; then he started out. The day was hot, and, because Coyote was always lazy, when he came to a nice, large shade tree, he thought he would lie down awhile. He threw down his bow and quiver and stretched out under the tree. Coyote was lying there looking up through the branches, and what do you think he saw? A great big fox!

"Oh!" said Coyote, "but I am lucky. I did not have to go hunting. I just came out here and lay under a tree, and there is my supper right over my head. Indeed I am lucky. Besides a good supper there is a fine fox skin up there for me.

"Oh, well, I guess I am just about the luckiest one in our tribe—besides being the best marksman, too. When I aim my arrows, I never miss. Just to prove it, I am going to take my five arrows and I will put the best arrow right here in the ground beside me, then I'll shoot one to the north, one to the south, one to the east, and one to the west."

So he did. He shot all his arrows away but one. He picked up the arrow he had put in the ground and said, "Now this is the arrow I am going to kill the fox with. But really, I am so good at shooting I don't even have to shoot with my hands. I am going to shoot this arrow with my toes."

All this time the poor fox was sitting up in the tree listening to Coyote tell how good he was at shooting, and he was nearly frightened to death. In fact, he was trembling so much he nearly fell out of the tree.

Coyote picked up his arrow, placed it between his toes, aimed it very carefully through the branches, and let it fly. But something happened and the arrow did not hit the fox. So, when the fox discovered he had not been shot, he jumped out of the tree and gleefully ran away. When he had reached a safe distance he called back, "Next time, Coyote, don't be so sure of yourself—and don't be so boastful!"

The Quails

(*Storyteller:* Have your listeners make a birdcall every time the word "quail" is used in the story. Teach them the kind of sound you would like them to make so their birdcalls don't disrupt the story.)

Ages ago a flock of more than a thousand quails lived together in a forest. They would have been happy, but they were in great dread of their enemy, the quail-catcher. He used to imitate the call of the quail, and when they gathered together in answer to it, he threw a great net over them, stuffed them into his basket, and carried them away to be sold.

Now one of these quails was very wise, and she said, "My friends, I've thought of a good plan. In the future, as soon as the quail-catcher throws his net over us, each one of you put your head through a mesh in the net and then all lift it up together and fly away with it. When we have flown far enough we can let the net drop on a thorn bush and escape from under it."

All agreed to her plan. The next day when the quail-catcher threw his net, the birds all lifted it together in the very way that the wise quail had told them, threw it on a thorn bush, and escaped. While the quail-catcher tried to free his net from the thorns, it grew dark, and he had to go home. This happened many times, till at last the quail-catcher's wife grew angry and asked her husband, "Why is it that you never catch any more quail?"

Then he said, "The trouble is that all the birds work together and help one another. If only they would quarrel, I could catch them fast enough."

A few days later, one of the quails accidentally stepped on the head of another quail as they landed on the feeding ground.

"Who stepped on my head?" the injured quail demanded.

"Don't be angry," the first quail replied. "I didn't mean to step on you."

But the other quail went on quarreling, and pretty soon blurted out, "I lifted all the weight of the net—you didn't help at all."

That made the first quail angry, and before long all were drawn into the argument. The quail-catcher was watching and saw his chance. He imitated the cry of the quail and cast his net over those who came together. They were still boasting and quarreling, and they did not help one another lift the net. So the hunter lifted the net himself and stuffed them into his basket.

But the wise quail gathered her friends together and flew far away, for she knew that quarrels are the root of misfortune.

Songs

Songs have a definite place in the Y-Indian Guide Programs. There are many songs that will fit into tribal meeting and Longhouse activities. Have fun by joining in an activity that crosses the generations. You can teach new songs at Longhouse workshops for parents, at special YMCA family events, or on camp-outs.

 # TIPS FOR THE SONG LEADER

A good song leader can make the tribal songfest a real treat. Children and parents respond to good music and appreciate someone who will help them sing well together. Try these ideas:

- Be enthusiastic; help members enjoy singing as they learn.
- Know the songs you are leading. Begin with one that most of the members know and enjoy.
- Sing along with the group and enjoy yourself.
- Give information about the background of the song.
- Make sure that the group hears the pitch. Don't start too high or too low.
- Give a firm starting signal and set and maintain the tempo of the song.
- Indicate when the group should sing loudly or softly and when to stop together!
- Use action songs when you want to provide movement and energetic involvement. Clapping, stamping feet, standing, and using hand motions all add zest to the occasion.

- Give clear, concise instructions for action songs. Repeat, if necessary, for better understanding.
- Use small, steady, rhythmic beats to guide the group. A broad, clear arm movement works best with large groups. Keeping the rhythm steady is a key to success.

Select songs appropriate for the meeting situation. Rousing choruses and action songs get parents and children off to a good start. Quiet songs have a great impact at campfires and tribal meetings just before the story or devotions.

The following songs are a few suggestions, but try other songs that the tribe enjoys. Take time to prepare, and, if possible, attend a singing skills workshop.

 # ACTION SONGS

The songs listed here are great fun and can be used in tribal meetings, hikes, camp-outs, and other group activities.

Damper Song

Oh, you push the damper in, (Arm forward)
And you pull the damper out, (Pull arm back)
And the smoke goes up the chimney just the same. (Fingers spiral up)
Just the same, just the same. (Full arm sweep right and left)
And the smoke goes up the chimney just the same.
(Repeat by whistling tune with motions, and on third verse, perform motions without noise.)

Deep and Wide

Deep and wide, deep and wide,
There's a fountain flowing deep and wide.
Deep and wide, deep and wide,
There's a fountain flowing deep and wide.
(Motions: Use hands in front to describe words:
Deep—one hand above the other
Wide—two palms facing each other
Fountain—both hands move upward
Flowing—hands move in waving motion)

Do Your Ears Hang Low?

Do your ears hang low? (Thumb in each ear)
Do they wobble to and fro? (Shake palms
   together)
Can you tie them in a knot? (Tie knot)
Can you tie them in a bow? (Tie bow at neck)
Can you throw them over your shoulder
Like a continental soldier? (Salute)
Do your ears hang low? (Repeat three times,
   each time faster.)

If You're Happy

(1)
If you're happy and you know it,
Clap your hands. (Clap, clap)
If you're happy and you know it,
Clap your hands. (Clap, clap)
If you're happy and you know it,
And you really want to show it,
If you're happy and know it,
Clap your hands. (Clap, clap)

(2)
If you're happy and you know it,
Stomp your feet. (Stomp, stomp)

(3)
If you're happy and you know it,
Shout "Hooray." (Hooray)

(4)
If you're happy and you know it,
Stand up. (Stand up)

(5)
If you're happy and you know it,
Do all four. (Clap, stomp, hooray, stand up)

Tommy Tinker

Little Tommy Tinker
Sat on a clinker
And he began to cry:
"Ma—a! Ma—a!"
Poor little innocent guy.
(Motions: Stand up while singing "Ma—a!" and
   then return to sitting position. Sing as a four-
   part round also.)

She'll Be Comin' Round the Mountain

(1)
She'll be comin' round the mountain when
she comes,
Toot, toot! (Pull cord)
She'll be comin' round the mountain when
she comes,
Toot, toot! (Pull cord)
She'll be comin' round the mountain, she'll
be comin' round the mountain, she'll be
comin' round the mountain when she
comes.

(2)
She'll be drivin' six white horses when she
comes,
Whoa-back! (Pull back reins)

(3)
Oh, we'll all go out to meet her when she
comes,
Hi, Babe! (Wave hands)

(4)
Oh, we'll kill the old red rooster when she
comes,
Hack, hack! (Chopping motion)

(5)
Oh, we'll all have chicken and dumplings
when she comes,
Yum, yum. (Rub tummy)

(6)
Oh, she'll wear her long red flannels when
she comes,
Scratch, scratch. (Scratch hip)

(7)
Oh, she'll have to sleep with Grandma when
she comes,
Snore, snore (Snore aloud)

The Cuckoo Song

(1)
Oh, I went to Peter's flowing spring
Where the water's so good,
And I heard there the cuckoo
As she called from the wood.

(Chorus)
Ho-li-ah, ho-le-rah-hi-hi-rah,
Ho-le-rah ku-kuck,
Ho-le-rah-ki-ki-ah, ho-le-rah-ku-kuck,
Ho-le-rah-ki-ki-ah, ho-le-rah-ku-kuck,
Ho-le-rah-ki-ki-ah, ho!

(2)
After Easter come sunny days
Then will melt all the snow;
Then I'll marry my maiden fair,
Who'll be happy, I know!

(Chorus)

(3)
When I've married my maiden fair,
What then can I desire?
Oh, a home for her tending
and some wood for the fire.

(Chorus)
(Motions: Drum knees on each syllable of "Ho-le-rah." Then slap knee on "Ho," clap hands on "le-rah," and snap fingers on "hi-hi-rah." Slap knee on "Ho," clap hands on "le-rah," and snap fingers on "ku-kuck.")

Bingo

There was a farmer had a dog and Bingo was
his name—o!
B-I-N-G-O, B-I-N-G-O, B-I-N-G-O, and Bingo
was his name—o!
There was a farmer had a dog and Bingo was
his name—o!
(Clap)-I-N-G-O, (clap)-I-N-G-O, (clap)-I-N-G-O,
and Bingo was his name—o!
(For each succeeding verse, eliminate one letter from Bingo and substitute a hand clap.)

Favorite Melodies

These songs are perennial favorites and are perfect for intergenerational meetings.

Are You Sleeping

Are you sleeping, are you sleeping,
Brother John, Brother John?
Morning bells are ringing,
Morning bells are ringing,
Ding, ding, dong,
Ding, ding, dong.
(Repeat as a four-part round.)

Take Me Out to the Ball Game

Take me out to the ball game,
Take me out to the crowd,
Buy me some peanuts and Cracker Jack,
I don't care if we never get back.
We will root-root-root for the home team;
If they don't win it's a shame.
For it's one-two-three strikes you're out
At the old ball game.

I've Been Working on the Railroad

I've been working on the railroad all the live-
long day.
I've been working on the railroad just to pass
the time away.
Don't you hear the whistle blowing? Rise up
so early in the morn.
Can't you hear the captain shouting? Dinah,
blow your horn.
Dinah, won't you blow—
Dinah, won't you blow—
Dinah, won't you blow your horn?
Dinah, won't you blow—
Dinah, won't you blow—
Dinah, won't you blow your horn?
Someone's in the kitchen with Dinah,
Someone's in the kitchen I know-o-o-o,
Someone's in the kitchen with Dinah
Strummin' on the old banjo. And singing—
Fee fi fiddle-i-o,
Fee fi fiddle-i-o-o-o-o,
Fee fi fiddle-i-o,
Strummin' on the old banjo.

Puffer Bellies

Down by the station early in the morning,
See the little puffer bellies all in a row.
See the engine driver turn the little handle.
Chug! Chug! Puff! Puff! Off they go!
(Melody may be sung in a four-part round.)

There Were Ten in a Bed

There were ten in the bed
And the middle one said,
"Roll over, roll over."
So they all rolled over
And one fell out.
There were nine in the bed (etc.)
(End)
There were none on the bed—GOODNIGHT!

The Grand Old Duke of York

The grand old Duke of York,
He had ten thousand men,
He marched them up the hill, and (Stand up)
He marched them down again. (Sit down)
And when they're up, they're up. (Stand up)
And when they're down, they're down. (Sit down)
And when they're only halfway up (Halfway— knees bent)
They're neither up nor down.

The More We Get Together

(Tune: "Ach Du Lieber Augustine")
The more we get together, together, together,
The more we get together, the happier we'll be.
For your friends are my friends, (Point to others)
And my friends are your friends. (Point to self)
The more we get together, the happier we'll be.
(Motions: Stand up when singing "together" or sit down if standing. Repeat song a second time for all to be seated.)

The Lord Said to Noah

(1)
The Lord said to Noah, "There's going to be a floody, floody."
The Lord said to Noah, "There's going to be a floody, floody.
Get your children out of the muddy, muddy,
Children of the Lord."

(Chorus)
So rise and shine and give God your glory, glory.
Rise and shine and give God your glory, glory.
Rise and shine and give God your glory, glory,
Children of the Lord.

(2)
The Lord said to Noah, "You better build an arky, arky."
The Lord said to Noah, "You better build an arky, arky.
Build it out of hickory barky, barky.
Children of the Lord."

(Chorus)

(3)
The animals, they came on, they came on by twosies, twosies,
The animals, they came on, they came on by twosies, twosies,
Elephants and kangaroosies, -roosies,
Children of the Lord.

(Chorus)

(4)
It rained and rained for forty days-y, days-y,
It rained and rained for forty days-y, days-y,
Almost drove those animals crazy, crazy,
Children of the Lord.

(Chorus)

(5)
The Lord said to Noah, "The flood is over, over,"
The Lord said to Noah, "The flood is over, over.
Get your children back to the clover, clover,
Children of the Lord."

(Chorus)

Hey, Ho! Nobody Home

Hey, ho! Nobody home.
Meat nor drink nor money have I none,
Yet I will be me-e-e-e-erry!
(Sing as three-part round.)

On Top of Old Smokey

(1)

On top of old Smokey
All covered with snow,
I learned a great lesson
All people should know.

(2)

For I met a brave hunter,
He was only a youth,
But he wasn't hunting rabbit,
He was hunting for truth.

(3)

And he told me he found it
In the red sunset glow,
In the sound of the thunder
And a touch of the snow.

(4)

And the truth was quite simple,
Just as plain as could be,
And I'll always remember
What the hunter told me.

(5)

Be fair to your neighbor,
Be honest and true,
Be kind to your neighbor
And he will be kind to you.

 FUN SONGS

The songs in this section can be used on trips and at meetings, and they are especially good for making new members feel welcome.

Animal Fair

I went to the animal fair, the birds and beasts
were there;

The big baboon by the light of the moon was
combing his long brown hair.
The monkey was a big lunk and sat on the
elephant's trunk;
The elephant sneezed, went down on his
knees,
And that was the end of the monk, the monk,
And that was the end of the monk.

Elle Ron

Elle Ron, Elle Ron, Elle Ron, Boom, Boom,
Boom,
Tum ba, Tum ba, Tum ba, Tum ba la la la
lai lai,
Tum ba la la la lai lai, Tum ba la la la LAI!

John Jacob Jingleheimer Schmidt

John Jacob Jingleheimer Schmidt—that's
my name, too.
Whenever we go out, the people always
shout,
There goes John Jacob Jingleheimer
Schmidt, Tra-la-la-la-la-la-la.
(Repeat four times, each time more softly except
for the ''tra-la-la-la-la.'')

Little Rabbit Hopping By

In a cabin in the wood
Little man by a window stood.
Saw a rabbit hopping by,
Knocking at his door.
"Help me, help me, sir," he said,
" 'fore the hunter shoots me dead."
"Come little rabbit, come inside,
Safely to abide."

Junior Birdmen

Up in the air, Junior Birdmen,
Up in the air, Birdmen, fly,
And when you hear that grand announcement,
That you have won your wings of tin,
Then you'll know the Junior Birdmen
Have sent their boxtops in.
It takes ten boxtops,
and five bottle bottoms.

Old MacDonald Had a Farm

(1)

Old MacDonald had a farm, ee-i-ee-i-o!
And on this farm he had some chicks, ee-i-ee-i-o!
With a chick, chick here and a chick, chick there,
Here a chick, there a chick,
Everywhere a chick, chick,
Old MacDonald had a farm, ee-i-ee-i-o!

(2)

Turkey . . . gobble, gobble

(3)

Cows . . . moo, moo

(4)

Horses . . . whinney

(5)

Dogs . . . arf, arf

(6)

Cats . . . meow, meow

(7)

Ducks . . . quack, quack

(8)

Ford . . . rattle, rattle

Row, Row, Row Your Boat

Row, row, row your boat
Gently down the stream.
Merrily, merrily, merrily, merrily,
Life is but a dream.
(Sing as a four-part round.)

Worms

Nobody loves me, everybody hates me,
Guess I'll eat some w-o-r-m-s.
(Chorus)
Long, slim, slimy ones,
Short, fat, juicy ones,
Itsy, bitsy, fuzzy, wuzzy w-o-r-m-s.

First you bite their heads off,
Then you chew their tails off,
Then you throw the rest a-w-a-y.
(Chorus)
Down goes the first one,
Down goes the second one,
Oh, how they wiggle and they s-q-u-i-r-m.
(Chorus)
Oops, comes the first one,
Oops, comes the second one,
Oh, how they wiggle and they s-q-u-i-r-m.
(Chorus)

This Old Man

(1)

This old man, he played one,
He played knick knack on my thumb.
(Chorus)
Knick knack, paddy whack, give a dog a bone,
This old man came rolling home.

(2)

This old man, he played two,
He played knick knack on my shoe.
(Chorus)

(3)

This old man, he played three,
He played knick knack on my knee.
(Chorus)

(4)

This old man, he played four,
He played knick knack on my door.
(Chorus)

(5)

This old man, he played five,
He played knick knack on my hive.
(Chorus)

(6)
This old man, he played six,
He played knick knack on my sticks.
(Chorus)

(7)
This old man, he played seven,
He played knick knack up in heaven.
(Chorus)

(8)
This old man, he played eight,
He played knick knack on my plate.
(Chorus)

(9)
This old man, he played nine,
He played knick knack on my spine.
(Chorus)

(10)
This old man, he played ten,
He played knick knack once again,
Knick knack, paddy whack, give a dog a
*   bone,*
Now we'll all go running home.

DEVOTIONAL SONGS

Devotional songs can be sung at the beginning or end of a meeting or around a campfire at the end of the day. They set a mood of reverence and reflection.

Do Lord

(1)
I've got a heavenly Father who hears and
*   answers prayers.*
I've got a heavenly Father who hears and
*   answers prayers.*
I've got a heavenly Father who hears and
*   answers prayers.*
Look away beyond the blue.

(Chorus, to be repeated after each verse)
Do, Lord, oh, do Lord, oh, do remember me.
Do, Lord, oh, do Lord, oh, do remember me.
Do, Lord, oh, do Lord, oh, do remember me.
Look away beyond the blue.

(2)
You can't wear the crown if you don't bear
*   the cross.*

(3)
I took Jesus as my Savior, you take him, too.

(4)
I've got a heavenly Father who hears and
*   answers prayers.*

Kum Bi Ya

(1)
Someone's cryin', Lord, Kum bi ya.
Someone's cryin', Lord, Kum bi ya.
Someone's cryin', Lord, Kum bi ya.
O Lord, Kum bi ya.

(Chorus, to be repeated after each verse)
Kum bi ya, my Lord, Kum bi ya.
Kum bi ya, my Lord, Kum bi ya.
Kum bi ya, my Lord, Kum bi ya.
O Lord, Kum bi ya.

(2)
Someone's prayin', Lord, Kum bi ya.

(3)
Someone's laughin', Lord, Kum bi ya.

(4)
Someone's singing, Lord, Kum bi ya.

O Great Spirit

(Tune: "Jesus, Lover of My Soul")

Oh, Great Spirit, now we part;
Enter into each one's heart.
Bless the fellowship we've had;
Follow us, each son and dad.

Taps

Day is done, gone the sun
From the lake, from the hills,
From the sky;
All is well, safely rest,
God is nigh.
Fading light dims the sight,
And a star gems the sky
Gleaming bright;
From afar, drawing nigh,
Falls the night.

PROGRAM SONGS

These songs are special to the Y-Indian Guide Programs. They can be used to help forge a strong identity among tribal members and reinforce the Y-Indian Guide Programs' aims.

Pals Forever

(Tune: "Clementine")

Pals Forever, Pals Forever,
That's our slogan, that's our song.
Boys are stronger, dads feel younger
When they take the boys along.
Moms are for it, dads adore it,
And the boys all think it's fine.
Pals Forever, Pals Forever,
As Indian Guides we'll have good times.
Through the days and through the years
We will wander side by side.
Pals Forever, Pals Forever,
The Great Spirit is our guide.

Pack the Sleeping Bags

(Tune: "Jingle Bells")

Pack the sleeping bags,
Get out the frying pan,
Shame on he who lags,
Whether boy or man.
We will have some fun,
Out where the coyotes wail;
Oh, dad and son will feel like one
When they're out on the trail.
(Chorus)
Indian Guides, Indian Guides
Happy as can be.
Indian Guides, Indian Guides
That's the club for me.
We'll take a hike
That's what we like,
Then home again go we.
Where dad and son have lots of fun,
That's where I want to be.

Indian Maiden Song

(Tune: "Clementine")

Friendship Always, Friendship Always,
That's our slogan, that's our code.
And we work and play together
As we travel on life's road.
Dads are for it, Moms adore it,
And the girls all think it's fine.
Friendship Always, Friendship Always,
Indian Maidens have good times.
Through the days and through the years
We will wander side by side.
Friendship Always, Friendship Always,
The Great Spirit as our guide.

Little Brave Chopping

(Tune: "Down at the Station")

Down at the tepees
Early in the morning,
See the Indian camp fires
Burning in a row.
Little brave is chopping
Wood for tepee fires.
Chop! Chop! Crack! Crack!
Watch him go.

Prayer Song

(Tune: "On Top of Old Smokey")

We come to the campfire,
Big braves with their boys.
"Pals Forever" our slogan,
We share many joys.
May the Great Spirit help us
To be clean, brave, and true
To families and neighbors
In all that we do.

Family Activities

Y-Indian Guide Programs help parents and children build a healthy, happy family life. The complex interaction of personalities within a family must be handled wisely if children are to grow into productive, self-confident adults. In many cases, parents enter the task of rearing children with little preparation.

This section of the manual is designed to offer resources in building effective communication and interaction among family members. The techniques provided here address both parents and children, outlining what both can do to help themselves and each other.

The first portion of this section describes an activity that tribe members can use at home to bring the family closer together and clarify personal values. It's called the *family circle*, and it is a simple way to get family members to talk about themselves and listen to each other. The second part is a collection of communication activities that parent-child teams can try during tribal meetings or on their own. These activities will help them learn more about each other and how they interact.

THE FAMILY CIRCLE

How would you describe the scene at your family dinner table? What is the room like? How does the table look? How many people usually sit at the table? Where do they sit? How fast is the meal eaten and finished? What is the conversation like? How would you describe the atmosphere? Which of the following situations occur too frequently to suit you?

- Everyone talks, no one listens. Stories go uncompleted, and interruptions are frequent.
- No one seems to have much to say. A heavy, sometimes tension-filled silence often hangs in the air.
- One person dominates the conversation. The knowledge that he or she may begin a long lecture or interrupt at any time puts a damper on the conversation.
- Everyone sits down and immediately begins eating. There's no sense of togetherness. Each person is in his or her own private world, except for passing the butter or answering a question.
- The parents' conversation is witty and lively. The children listen obediently but are rarely included in the conversation, except occasionally to answer a question posed by the parents.
- Everyone begins eating so fast that there's no time to appreciate the food—its look, smell, or taste.
- Every discussion turns into an argument. No one seems to want or know how to hear the other person's point of view.
- The children dash away from the table as soon as they are finished eating. They don't feel there is anything worth staying for.

These situations occur so often; not in every home and not all the time in any one home, yet often enough. Parents and children rarely express it, but all want the family mealtime to be more special than it is—more fun, more caring, more interesting.

No one technique can completely change a family's way of relating to each other. Caring, helping, and listening cannot be simulated or learned overnight. They are attitudes and skills that take years to develop. Nevertheless, there *is* something that families can begin doing today that will help them grow closer together, make the family meal more lively and interesting, and help each member become clearer about his or her own values and sense of identity. It's called the *family circle*.

Family circle is really a very simple procedure. First, after all the food is placed on the table and everyone is seated, everyone holds hands around the table. One member of the family, *not necessarily a parent*, suggests a topic or question that would be interesting for each person to think about and then to share with the others. For example, the daughter might say, "Everyone think of the nicest thing that happened to you today." (Other family circle topics are suggested later.)

With eyes closed, still holding hands, each person ponders the question or topic suggested. When a person thinks of something—in this case a nice thing that happened—he or she squeezes the hand of the person to the right and left. After a half-minute or so, even if everyone has not thought of something, people drop hands, open their eyes, and proceed to help themselves to dinner. (Families who want to say a formal prayer, in addition to the family circle, can do so either before the topic is suggested or before people begin eating.) Then, one by one, each member of the family volunteers his or her response to the question or topic that was raised.

Everyone should feel free to be silent if they do not care to share thoughts; no one should feel bad about not being able to think of something to say on a given topic. Some people speak up more easily than others, however, and it is often helpful to draw out the quieter members by asking, for example, "Susie, what was the nicest thing that happened to *you* today?"

Each person gets a turn. If Susie is describing her day, then Mom doesn't come in with a story of her own at this point. She and the others hear Susie out and ask her questions, if they wish. They don't argue or disagree with her, either. For example, if Susie has just finished telling how a particular compliment she received about her clothes was the nicest thing that happened to her that day, another member should not chime in, "Ugh, that doesn't sound nice at all! That sounds like an insult to me." When a person is the focus of attention, his or her thoughts and feelings are listened to and accepted—that's all. Later on there is time for disagreement or free discussion.

How long each person has the focus of the family depends a great deal on the question posed, the size of the family, the ages of the children, the ability of the children to listen to one another, the general mood of the family on that particular night, and so on. Whether they take two minutes or fifteen minutes for their family circle, each family usually establishes its own norms about time limits, and these are usually quite flexible.

As soon as each member of the family who wants the focus has shared a response, then the family can continue with a free discussion. Members can say, "You know, Susie, the same compliment that made you feel good would have offended me," or "When you told your story, Jerry, it made me think of something that once happened to me." The conversation may even go in an entirely new direction.

Topics for a family circle are infinite. The only requirements are that

- they should be topics about which most members of the family are likely to have something to say;
- they should be questions or issues for which there are no right answers;
- they should clarify values, and should be thought-provoking, interesting, or just plain fun to consider.

To illustrate the variety of family circle topics, a list of topics is provided below. However, you can draw some of the best questions and topics from the lives of your own family members.

Sample Family Circle Topics
- What is one thing you'd like to learn how to do?
- Can you recall one of the best meals you've ever had, here or anywhere else?
- What is a funny story you heard or a funny thing that happened to you recently?
- What is something you'd like to do this coming weekend (Christmas, summer, etc.)?

- What was the best thing that happened at school or work today?
- (*Anytime, but definitely at Thanksgiving*) What are you thankful for?
- (*At any holiday*) What does this holiday mean to you?
- What is your earliest memory (or memories)?
- Who is your best friend? What do you like about him or her?
- What is some question you've been wondering about?
- Who is (was) the best teacher you have (had)? What do (did) you like about him or her?
- Where is your favorite spot to be by yourself?
- What is your favorite book (poem, TV show, kind of music, tree, flower, sport)?
- What animal are you most like?
- What is something you wish for that would help someone you know?

How often should the family circle be done? There is really no one answer. In some families it can work almost every night, with many topics repeated frequently and many created by the family members for different occasions. Other families prefer to have a circle once a week, when guests come, or on holidays. There is no correct frequency; each family needs to experiment to discover its own best pattern.

The family meal need not be a battleground, disaster area, or morgue. It can be filled with interesting conversation in which members actually listen to one another. It can be a time when family members get to know one another better, and values are clarified and important issues are considered.

COMMUNICATION ACTIVITIES

How well do you communicate with your child? Do you listen to each other? Do you share? Effective communication is one of the most difficult skills to learn, but when we learn it well, the benefits show up in many areas of our lives.

Communication means saying what you mean, hearing what others have to say, listening, and sharing. You have probably found that on some days and with some people you communicate better than on other days and with other people. What makes the difference? Perhaps it's your mood or the weather. Perhaps it's how you are being treated by that other person. Or perhaps it's the topic under discussion. Whatever the reason, awareness of how you're communicating is one giant step toward developing your communication skills.

The following activities are designed to help both parents and children engage in various kinds of communication. Some activities require group participation, but most of the activities are for parent and child to do alone together with minimal group discussion. You may find yourselves talking about topics you've never discussed before. You'll probably learn something about yourself as well as your child. Regardless, you'll both benefit from the shared experience and grow in your communication skills.

Before you begin, read the ground rules listed below and make sure everyone understands them. Then, try doing one activity or perhaps two at a meeting or camp-out. Be sure to allow time for the pairs to have a discussion at the end of each activity. Questions for them to think about might be "What did you learn?" and "How did you feel about the activity?"

Good luck and have fun talking with each other!

Ground Rules

1. Listen to each other.
2. Speak for yourself.
3. Avoid put-downs.
4. Say what you mean.
5. Be responsible for yourself.

Group Activities

These activities require the participation of the whole tribe, although parts of them may be done by parent-child teams alone.

Name Tags

Purpose: To get acquainted and to share some information about each other.

Materials: 5" x 7" cards; pencils, markers, or crayons; safety pins or tape.

1. Give each person a card and a pencil, marker, or crayon.
2. Ask each person to do the following (one at a time). If the children in your group are nonwriters, have them draw their responses.
   - Write your name somewhere on the card.
   - In one corner write the town where you were born.
   - In another corner write your favorite food.
   - In another corner write the names of two or three friends.
   - In another corner write the name of a place you like.
   - Lightly color the card your favorite color.
3. Have them walk around the room looking at the cards of others and talking with them about their responses.
4. Ask the group to pair off, each with someone he or she didn't know well at the beginning.
5. Have everyone sit in a circle. Have each partner introduce the other person to the entire group using the information on the card.

Respect

Purpose: To understand and discuss the value of respect, to explore reasons why people are respected, and to discuss ways in which respect is earned.

Materials: Paper, pencils.

1. As a group, define the word *respect*. This is especially important if you have very young children in the group.
2. On your own sheet of paper, list five people for whom you have respect. Then, next to each name, explain why you respect that person.
3. Share your list with others and discuss.
4. On your sheet of paper, list five reasons why you want other people to respect you.
5. Share your list with others when completed.
6. On your sheet of paper, list ten things you can do to be respected by others and by your child or parent.
7. Share and discuss your list when completed.

Getting It All Together

Purpose: To share information in the group about home responsibilities, to discuss the responsibilities without becoming emotional and to consider change or flexibility in home responsibilities.

Materials: Newsprint, marker, paper, pencils.

1. Begin with a group discussion of the home responsibilities of both parents and children. List these on newsprint so they are easier to recall in the next step.
2. Have the group members pair off into actual parent-child teams. Using the large group list, ask each team to list their individual home responsibilities in two columns, much like the large group list.
3. Next to each item on the list note what happens when that responsibility is not carried out. For example: "Mow lawn—grass goes to seed, neighbors complain, insects breed."
4. Put an "X" by the least favorite responsibilities or the ones that are often forgotten.
5. Discuss the items with an "X."
   a. Are they necessary?
   b. In what way could they be changed?
   c. Who else could do them?
   d. Could the responsibility for them be rotated in the family?
6. Come to some agreement and plan of action for the "X-ed" items.

Surprise!

Purpose: To work together and to share with others.

Materials: This will vary with each parent-child pair. You may want to have handy items such as brown bags, songbooks, glue, magazines, and scissors.

1. Parent and child as partners are to spend five minutes talking about something they could do or make for someone else. Many choices are available for that someone else: family, relatives, neighbors, the other parent, another parent-child pair in the group, and so on.
2. After five minutes, have each pair begin to plan and execute their project. Some may need to go outside for items; others may need the assistance of other parent-

child teams in order to carry out their plan.

3. Arrange a time span in which to carry out the projects, perhaps the two weeks until the next meeting.

4. After the projects or plans are completed and delivered, discuss as a group the feelings associated with working out a plan and delivering it. Did you plan well? Did both of you have a part in the plan? What happened when you delivered your project? How did you feel?

Parent-Child Team Activities

The following activities are meant for parent-child teams alone. They can be used both during tribal meetings and at home.

Talking Up and Talking Down

Purpose: To show how physical positions affect communication, to give parents a child's-eye view of the world, and to give children an adult's-eye view of the world.

Materials: A sturdy chair for each pair to stand on.

1. Decide which one of you will be A and which B. A should stand on the chair and B should sit on the floor directly in front of A. Try to maintain eye contact. Talk about how this feels. (Allow two minutes.)

   Then change places, with B standing on the chair and A sitting down. Talk with each other about how this feels. (Allow two minutes.)

2. B should reach down and take A's hand and hold it for a few seconds, then reach down and give A a pat on the head. Talk about how this feels. (Allow time.)

   Change positions and try the same things: A and B should make hand contact. A should give B's arm a little yank, then reach down and give B a pat on the head.

3. Now sit at the same level but back to back and carry on a conversation. How does this position feel?

4. Now stand up but stand about ten feet apart and talk. Any change in the conversation?

5. Do what you need to do now to get comfortable and in a good position for talking. Talk about what you felt during the experience. Talk about how your body feels in the position you are in now. What have you learned about the effect of body position on communication? (Allow two minutes.)

Birthday Party

Purpose: To give parents and children an opportunity to talk about friends and what they mean.

Materials: None.

1. Pretend that you and your child are each going to have a birthday party. Begin by asking your child whom he or she thinks should be invited to your party and why. Then share whom you would invite and why.

2. Now reverse the process. Have your child ask you whom you think should be invited to the child's party and why. Your child should then share whom he or she would invite and why.

3. Talk about the following questions:

   a. Why have a party?
   b. Why is it fun to have friends?
   c. What does it mean to be a friend?
   d. When is it hard to be a friend?

If I Could . . .

Purpose: To allow parent and child to daydream and to share dreams and hopes together.

Materials: None.

1. Sit quietly with your eyes closed for 3 minutes and think of dreams and hopes. Think of topics related to the following:

   "If I could, I would like my family to . . ."
   "If I could, I would like to be . . ."
   "If I could, I would like to visit . . ."
   "If I could, I would like my brother/sister/ husband/wife to . . ."
   (Allow 3 minutes.)

2. Share your thoughts with each other. Take enough time to recall as many of your thoughts as possible.

3. Share some insights you had about each other. You may find that this activity will bring up some topics that will be useful for further discussion at home.

Silent Acting

Purpose: To give parent and child an opportunity to act out each other's roles in a make-believe situation while the other person guesses what is being acted out.

Materials: None, or as needed to play the other person.

Each of you takes a turn acting out a situation silently. The idea is to mimic the other person while he or she watches and tries to guess what is being acted out.

ACT I—Child acts out the parent's role.

1. Pick out a situation or an incident between you and your parent that happens a lot.
2. Think of how your parent reacts in that situation.
3. Silently, using facial, hand, or other body expressions, movements, and positions, act out how your parent might react to you in that situation. *Do not use words.*
4. When you're finished, your parent tries to guess what you have acted, including

   - the situation,
   - possible feelings you were trying to show,
   - possible words that might have been said or felt, and
   - why that situation and your reaction to it was chosen.

5. Briefly discuss how that experience was for each of you.

   - How did you feel about the play acting, watching, and guessing?
   - In real life how do each of you feel in those situations?
   - What were the possible feelings your parent was having?
   - If needed, what can be done to change the situation?

Act II—Parent acts out the child's role. Follow steps 1 through 5 as described above and silently mimic your child in a situation or recent incident.

Have fun doing this. It might not seem easy at first. However, as you get into it, you'll find it is fun and offers a chance for each of you to express yourself in a different way to one another.

How Will You Know if I Don't Tell You?

Purpose: To give parent and child a chance to share some things they really like about each other that maybe they have wanted to say, but never have said.

Materials: Paper or large blank card, pencils.

1. On your own piece of paper or a large card draw the following tic-tac-toe figure. Draw it quite large.

2. In the top-left box write the initials of your best friend.
3. In the top-center box list 4-6 things (behavior, traits, characteristics, etc.) you really like about that best friend.
4. In the middle-left box write the initials of your parent/child.
5. In the middle-center box list 4-6 things (behavior, traits, characteristics, etc.) you really like about your parent/child.
6. In the bottom-left box write your own initials.
7. In the bottom-center box list 4-6 things (behavior, traits, characteristics, etc.) you really like about yourself.
8. In the top-right box and middle-right box, next to the list of things you really like, put a check mark if you have told that person in the last 2 weeks that you like that thing about him or her. Put a 0 if you haven't.
9. In the bottom-right box put a check mark in the box if you have been told by someone in the last 2 weeks that he or she really likes that thing about you that is on your list of things you like about yourself. Put a 0 if you haven't been told.

Finally, when both of you have finished your individual charts, share with each other what you have written. The goal is not only to share, but also to discover something new about yourselves and how you feel when you tell or are told something you really like. It may also encourage you to tell and share with another person (e.g., friend, parent, child) the things you really like more often.

My Favorites

Purpose: To allow parent and child to share information about themselves, to learn about each other, and to learn about themselves.

Materials: Paper, pencils.

1. List on the paper all the different kinds of favorite things you can think of; for example, food, drink, sports, TV shows, clothes, shoes, colors, cars, places, kinds of transportation, friends, books, summer activities, or winter activities.
2. Next to each item, put an "X" if it has been a favorite for a long time and an "O" if it is a new favorite.
3. Share your lists with each other. Go through each list slowly and add to each item how you think it got to be your favorite.
4. Briefly discuss the experience.
   a. What did you learn about the favorites on your partner's list?
   b. Were there any surprises?
5. This entire activity may be repeated for least favorites too!

I Want From You . . .

Purpose: To list "wants," to share and decide what can be done together and individually about wants, and to increase understanding and good feelings in the parent-child relationship.

Materials: Paper, pencils.

1. Each of you should draw on a sheet of paper the illustration shown below and write in the headings.
2. Each of you should then do the following steps separately:
   a. In the "I want from you" column, list 5 things you want from the other person that you don't feel you're getting enough of at present. For example, your child wants you to play backgammon (or another game) more often; you want your child to do agreed-upon household chores on time.
   b. In the next column, "When? or How often?" complete what you would like to happen. For example, your child wants to play backgammon (or another game) once a week; you want chores done on the agreed-upon schedule once a week.
   c. In the "How important is it to me?" column, rank items listed in order of their importance to you. Most important is 1, next is 2, and so on down to the least important one on your list.
3. Share your lists and responses. When each of you has shared, use the last col-

"I Want From You _____"	When? or How Often?	How Important Is It To Me?	What WE Decide To Do About It
1)			
2)			
3)			
4)			
5)			

umn, "What we decided to do about it," to fill in your decision on each issue.

Parent-Child Conversations

Purpose: To help parent and child become aware of the need to listen and share how they feel about certain issues.

Materials: Paper, crayons.

1. One of you should make a short statement about one of the topics listed below. The other partner will then ask several questions, each beginning with "Do you mean?" These questions can only be answered yes or no. When 3 yes answers have been given, switch.
2. The following are some topics you might like to discuss. Be sure to vary these topics so that they are appropriate to your needs.
   a. Cooperation
   b. Sharing
   c. Friends
   d. I like to do things with you because . . .
   e. Being afraid
   f. Love
3. After 2 topics or 10 minutes, stop. Each of you should then draw a picture of something you just talked about. Tell your partner about your picture.
4. Alternative: Instead of drawing a picture, share "I learned" statements with each other:
   a. I learned that I . . .
   b. I was surprised that I . . .
   c. I was pleased that I . . .

Family Life Mural

Purpose: To provide opportunities to share important things about the family.

Materials: Brown mural paper or grocery bags, tape, crayons.

1. Take a piece of large brown paper or cut open several grocery bags and tape them together. Sit down as a team and, working together, draw a picture of the following:
   a. What our family looks like
   b. Our family's favorite place
   c. A way we work together as a family
   d. A way we play together as a family
2. Allow time for each of you to share what it is you added to the mural and why.
3. If possible, hang the mural in a visible

place at the gathering or display it at home.

Feelings Jar

Purpose: To open up communication between parent and child regarding feelings, to practice talking about feelings, and to label feelings.

Materials: Wide-mouthed jar (or can or bowl), small slips of paper, pencil.

1. Take a jar, can, or bowl (with a mouth wide enough for an adult's hand to get all the way in) and label this the Feelings Jar. Many feeling words are included on the list below. Write each word on a separate slip of paper and place them all in the jar.

Feeling Words

pleased	impatient
surprised	encouraged
embarrassed	weary
happy	hurt
wonderful	lost
flustered	afraid
comfortable	bugged
glad	cheated
nervous	annoyed
excited	worried
bored	hopeful
put upon	confident
satisfied	eager
fed up	

2. One of you should pick a slip of paper from the jar. The two of you should then discuss the following questions:
   a. Did anyone in our family have that feeling during the week?
   b. When? What were the circumstances at the time?
   c. How does that member of the family feel about the situation now?
   d. When the family member had that feeling, what could have happened that would have made that person feel differently?
3. Repeat the process, with the other partner's removing a slip from the jar.
4. You might take this activity home to do as a family. It's a great way to make it OK to talk about feelings.

Appendix

This appendix contains additional resources for Y-Indian Guide Programs.

American Indian Culture

The following addresses are resources for information concerning American Indian culture, issues, and concerns.

Bureau of Indian Affairs Area Offices

Aberdeen Area Office
115 Fourth Avenue, S.E.
Aberdeen, SD 57401

Albuquerque Area Office
5301 Central Avenue, N.E.
Albuquerque, NM 87198

Anadarko Area Office
Box 368
Anadarko, OK 73005

Billings Area Office
316 North 26th Street
Billings, MT 59101

Eastern Area Office
Broyhill Building
1000 North Glebe Road
Arlington, VA 22201

Juneau Area Office
Box 3-8000
Juneau, AK 99802

Minneapolis Area Office
15 South Fifth Street
Minneapolis, MN 55402

Muskogee Area Office
Federal Building
Muskogee, OK 74401

Navajo Area Office
Window Rock, AZ 86515

Phoenix Area Office
Box 7007
Phoenix, AZ 85011

Portland Area Office
1425 N.E. Irving Street
Portland, OR 97208

Sacramento Area Office
2800 Cottage Way
Sacramento, CA 95825

American Indian Organizations

American Indian Historical Society
1493 Masonic Avenue
San Francisco, CA 94117

American Indian Movement (AIM)
1209 Fourth Street S.E.
Minneapolis, MN 55414

National Congress of American Indians
804 D Street N.E.
Washington, DC 20002

National Indian Youth Council
318 Elm Street
S.E. Albuquerque, NM 87102

National Tribal Chairman's Association
818 18th Street N.W. Suite 840
Washington, DC 20006

Sources for Craft Materials

Addresses for craft material suppliers and a description of their specialties follow.

Berman Leather Craft
145 South Street
Boston, MA 02111-2882
1-800-341-3274

Leathercraft supplies. Write for catalog.

Boin Arts and Crafts Company
87 Morris Street
Morristown, NJ 07960-0659
201-539-0600

Various craft materials. Write for catalog.

Craft Kits
P.O. Box 253
Urbana, IL 61801
217-384-1112

Simple Indian kits for tribal meetings. Includes peacepipe, tomahawk, necklace, drum, arm and ankle bands, and tepee, among other projects. Some assembled products. Write for catalog.

Grey Owl
P.O. Box 507
113-15 Springfield Boulevard
Queens Village, NY 11429
718-464-9300

Supply great Indian theme kits already assembled, as well as literature. Write for catalog.

Indy Products
1225 North Indianapolis Road
Mooresville, IN 46158
317-831-1114

Pine car derby racers.

J & A Handy Crafts, Inc.
210 Front Street
Hempstead, NY 11550
516-292-1220

Distributor of craft and school supplies. Write for catalog.

Mastercraft Jewelry & Design
11609 Martens River Circle
Fountain Valley, CA 92708
714-549-7136

Jewelry making kits.

Pack O'Fun
14 Main Street
Park Ridge, IL 60068

Various craft supplies and magazines. Write for catalog.

Pinecar & Woodland Scenics
1 Main Street
Linn Creek, MO 65052
314-346-5555

Pine car derby racers.

S & S Arts and Crafts
Colchester, CT 06415
203-537-3451

Distributor of kits and craft supplies for all ages. Write for catalog.

Triarco Arts and Crafts
14650 28th Avenue North
Plymouth, MN 55441
1-800-328-3360

Group projects available at low prices. Used by many day camps. Write for catalog.

True to Nature, Inc.
104 East Vine Street
Hatfield, PA 19440
215-362-7789

Wooden snap-together birdhouses, feeders, key racks, etc.

Woodkrafter Kits, Inc.
P.O. Box 808
Yarmouth, ME 04096
207-846-3746

Wood projects.

National Y-Indian Guide Center

The Frank Phillips Foundation, Inc., owns and operates the National Y-Indian Guide Center as part of WOOLAROC Museum and Wildlife Preserve, located 14 miles southwest of Bartlesville, Oklahoma, on Highway 123. It is open to the public, and Y-Indian Guide Program parents and children will find it well worth visiting. The Museum has a large collection of Western art, and the Y-Indian Guide Center includes Heritage Hall, an information center that includes authentic Indian exhibits; Enchanted Walkway, with trailside displays of native Oklahoma trees, flowers, fossils, and minerals; and Thunderbird Canyon Nature Trails. For further information contact Blue Hill Townsend, WOOLAROC, Route 3, Bartlesville, Oklahoma 74003, (918) 336-0307.

Additional Resources for Your Y-Indian Guide Programs

See the YMCA Program Store Catalog for details about these additional items for Y-Indian Guide Programs or contact the Program Store, Box 5077, Champaign, IL 61820, (217) 351-5077.

4930 Friends Always: The *New* Y-Indian Guide Programs Manual (176 pp) $9.00

New Y-Indian Guide Programs Tribal Kits (includes 10 copies of *Friends Always: The New Y-Indian Guide Programs Manual*, 20 emblems, 20 cloth headbands, and a Program Charter)

4940 New Y-Indian Guides Tribal Kit $98.00

4941 New Y-Indian Braves Tribal Kit $98.00

4942 New Y-Indian Princesses Tribal Kit $98.00

4943 New Y-Indian Maidens Tribal Kit $98.00

4657 Y-Indian Guide Programs Leaders Manual (36 pp) $8.00

4919 Indian Tales That Teach (80 pp) $7.50

4485 Y-Indian Guide Programs Charter $.50

852 Programs Recruitment Resource Kit $50.00

436 Y-Indian Guide Programs Emblem $1.85
4076 Y-Indian Guides Chevron $1.60
4077 Y-Indian Braves Chevron $1.60
4078 Y-Indian Maidens Chevron $1.60
4079 Y-Indian Princesses Chevron $1.60

Y-Indian Guides

1281 Cloth Headband 10/$13.00
1282 Paper Headband 100/$4.25
697 Traditional Emblem 10/$12.00

Y-Indian Princesses

1284 Cloth Headband 10/$13.00
1285 Paper Headband 100/$4.25
745 Traditional Emblem 10/$13.00

Y-Indian Maidens

1283 Cloth Headband 10/$13.00
744 Traditional Emblem 10/$12.00

Y-Indian Braves

1287 Cloth Headband 10/$13.00
820 Traditional Emblem 10/$12.00

Resources for Y-Trail Programs

4894 Y-Trail Programs Manual (64 pp) $7.00
576 Y-Trail Blazers Charter $.30
4552 Trail Program Recruitment Audio/Visual $65.00

Y-Trail Programs Embroidered Emblems

752 Y-Trail Blazers Emblem $1.60
817 Y-Trail Maidens Emblem $1.60
818 Y-Trail Mates Emblem $1.60

819 Y-Coed Trail Blazers Emblem $1.60

438 Y-Trail Maidens Chevron $1.60
440 Y-Trail Mates Chevron $1.60
442 Y-Trail Blazers Chevron $1.60
4075 Y-Coed Trail Blazers Chevron $1.60

(See the Program Store Catalog for a complete listing of Y-Trail Awards available.)

Prices shown are subject to change.